PENGUIN BOOKS

LITTLE DROPS

Born and bred in Singapore, Theresa W. Devasahayam is a family and gender anthropologist. At a young age, her interest in women's issues was ignited when she discovered her mother's story of adoption. As an undergraduate, she enjoyed sociology and anthropology and furthered her interest in gender studies at the graduate level when she completed her PhD at Syracuse University in the USA. During her career, Theresa has edited seven books and co-authored one book, mostly academic and concerned with various facets of women's lives—all having one connecting thread in that they ask fundamental questions around inequality, oppression, and exploitation between the sexes. This is her first book written primarily for a non-academic audience. With the same passion she puts into her writing, Theresa enjoys engaging in various charity efforts aimed at raising funds for girls' and women's empowerment projects in developing countries. Her aspirations are simple: give back to society whatever gifts one may have, recognizing that one has been empowered to empower others.

ADVANCE PRAISE FOR *LITTLE DROPS: CHERISHED CHILDREN OF SINGAPORE'S PAST*

'The author, an anthropologist known for exploration of issues of inequality, oppression, and sexual exploitation, has here produced a poignant historical record, an oral history of recollections by fifteen adoptees (with one exception, girls of Chinese descent) of their apparent abandonment by birth parents and their subsequent fates in adoptive families from diverse ethnic, religious, and socio-economic backgrounds. In a series of deceptively straightforward storytelling, Devasahayam has created absorbing narratives of transformation from a child's ill fortune to collective acts of redemptive love. The stories of cross-cultural adoption from Singapore's recent past, covering the years between the 1930s and 1970s, before changes in adoption law prohibited adoption of a child from outside one's ethnic group came into force, are told from the point of view of the adoptees but also bring into the narratives the perspectives of adoptive parents and members of their social circle as well as of birth parents, where they could be traced, and of go-betweens facilitating transfer of a child.

What makes these stories so poignant? What makes them significant beyond the undoubtedly intrinsic value of individual biography? According to the author, the opportunity to tell their stories became an opportunity to fill a gap in the collective memory of Singaporeans, to tell of 'lives, experiences, and challenges' in the words of those who were uniquely granted a lifeline of hope when ethno-religious markers of identity were not yet formalized markers of separation.

The poignancy of this volume lies in life stories that reflect the social and political volatility of Singapore society under Japanese occupation and during pre-independence. They reflect the precarious existence of marginalized peoples that found its starkest expression in the giving away of one's own child to other families, compelled by economic necessity but, we are told, motivated by values of altruism and care for the child and indeed for the wider family. Recognition of, and attention to, emotional costs borne by birth parents add necessary insights to ample scholarship on commerce of traffic in children in East Asian and Southeast Asian regions during the early twentieth century.

Thus, these biographies evoke in vivid detail the trajectories of individual lives of adoptees, of their identities and contrastive fates shaped in the intersections of class, race, family moral codes, religious ritual life, gender norms, and emotional culture: importantly, adoptive parents' capacity for affection as well as material care. Diverse socio-economic circumstances and ethno-cultural contexts make for disparate experiences of adoption, but what these accounts have in common is a quest to belong, the yearning for kinship ties that afford stability and security of identity as well as recognition of worth. What makes these stories more widely significant is that however accounts differ in certain respects, they have in common, overwhelmingly so, emphatically non-commercial, non-transactional dimensions, and principled conduct under pressure. During times of acute crisis, support for a child is sought predominantly from trusted relatives or acquaintances, concern is for a stable and sustainable future of the child, and admission into a family unit is recalled by adoptees as a process of sustained care and affection. These are richly textured narratives, reflecting the multi-cultural and multi-ethnic composition of Singaporean society, and they are brought to life through sharing of subjective experiences of adoptees who combine gratitude for opportunities to thrive with sober recognition of the inequalities at the heart of their stories.

It is thus enlightening to read that when it came to disclosure of identity of birth parents, always a turning point in the lives of adoptees, when belonging and truth and trust are in crisis, individual adoptees in most cases chose to make decisions based on emotional truth. That is, overriding the disclosure of biological birth, of their ethnic and cultural origin, even of concealment of their birth by some adoptive parents, they chose to acknowledge and, in their reminiscences, pay tribute to, their adoptive parents' story of care and love which crossed, and challenged, ethnic and cultural boundaries.

Arguably, in this way, their stories enter the national narrative of the making of Singapore society, providing an oral history of the changing relationship between State and citizens, and thus a very particular historical lens through which to view the making of its citizenry. The record of a period of Singaporean social history now past allows an insight into the impact of State legislation on adoption which has come to shape classification of social identity along defined lines of ethnicity.'

—Professor Maria Jaschok,
Oxford School of Global & Area Studies,
University of Oxford

'*Little Drops* is an enjoyable read, at its easiest. At its hardest, it poses challenges on how far we have come in: valuing the intricacies of family relationships and structures; not being prejudicial on what is the 'unlike'; embracing differences; being anti-racist; facing and accepting a global world where couples adopt children from other cultures or that children are born to parents in inter-ethnic marriages. This book demands a 'Pause' for reflection and self-inspection as we get into the lives of fifteen adopted children who are today in their 50s and beyond. A timely story that is finally being told.

The book's narratives showcase the adoption of Chinese girls and boys by Indian or Malay parents for various reasons— superstition, astrological beliefs, poverty, patriarchy, deaths, fear of Japanese soldiers targeting Chinese. These adoptions took place as couples wanted children, loved children, out of empathy, for good luck, and because they might have lost children. What is unsaid in the stories but a comforting reflection is just this—none were stumped by the fact that a Chinese girl or boy was going to grow up in an Indian or Malay home; it was just acceptance or a pragmatism that a child is going to be raised as their own, adoptively.

Devasahayam's interviews and writing provide a detailed collation of stories of adaptation, loyalty, love, acculturised girls and boys who were raised in wholesome environments of love, nurture, acceptance and discipline. The constant derailment stemmed from not knowing openly and directly that they were adopted or in not having the skills to cope with that to continue remaining confident, wanted and loved. Unthinking careless remarks did produce spasms of anxiety and insecurity when the adopted child was already culturally, linguistically, religiously and food-wise attuned to and in sync with adoptive families.

Little Drops unveils the world of an adopted child in a historical space of time, land, cultures, religion, rituals aiming to showcase the intersections between self-identity, self-empowerment, acceptance and adaptations to stable environments of love and security. Almost all the stories show a more glowing account of how adoption had worked for them in school, in work life, in relationships and in becoming themselves. One vivid turbulence is captured in the last chapter as the adopted child discovers very much later as an adult that he is actually a Chinese who was adopted by a Malay family and had grown up all his life thinking he was Malay. The pain of that discovery also meant an introspection on family relations, values, acceptance of one's origins or ethnicity and a re-assembling one's identity in a more self-directed way.

Paradoxically, in the epilogue, Devasahayam tells us that the law now does not allow for inter-cultural adoptions. Yet here is *Little Drops* showcasing that despite its flaws, the children grew up well in good relationships of care, love, security and are contributors to our society.'

—Braema Mathi, researcher,
writer, and social activist from Singapore

'*Little Drops* provides a unique bottom-up perspective on Singaporean society by recounting a long-neglected socio-cultural phenomenon from its recent past. It is an incredible story of multicultural lives and cross-cultural entanglements in the city-state seen from the perspective of adoptive children born from the 1930s to the early 1970s. It is touching, inspiring, and educative all at the same time. The stories of fifteen children are told with insight of an ethnographer and written in an intimate style of a biographer. The rich fabric of Singapore's inter-ethnic relationship, the support mechanism at the societal level, and the blending of people from different cultural spheres are vividly narrated in these stories. This fabulous book is a significant contribution to the history of Singapore and is key to understanding its multicultural heritage.'

—Professor Tansen Sen, Center for Global Asia,
New York University, Shanghai

Little Drops

Cherished Children
of Singapore's Past

Theresa W. Devasahayam

PENGUIN BOOKS

An imprint of Penguin Random House

PENGUIN BOOKS

USA | Canada | UK | Ireland | Australia
New Zealand | India | South Africa | China | Southeast Asia

Penguin Books is part of the Penguin Random House group of companies
whose addresses can be found at global.penguinrandomhouse.com

Published by Penguin Random House SEA Pte Ltd
9, Changi South Street 3, Level 08-01,
Singapore 486361

First published in Penguin Books by Penguin Random House SEA 2023

ISBN 9789815127126

Typeset in Adobe Garamond Pro by MAP Systems, Bengaluru, India

www.penguin.sg

To my grandmother, Grace Imelda Joseph,
for her love, inner beauty, and strength,
and her dedication towards raising my mother, Jane Felicia.
And to all my respondents without whom this book
would not have been possible.

Contents

Chapter 1: On Adoption: A Collective Memory   1

Chapter 2: The Love of Children   8

Chapter 3: Half-Eurasian   18

Chapter 4: Two Families to Call Home   26

Chapter 5: What's in a Name?   39

Chapter 6: The Intermediary   52

Chapter 7: The Indian Sister   62

Chapter 8: The Woman I Am   78

Chapter 9: The Blue Bag   90

Chapter 10: Then There Were Two   100

Chapter 11: Trustworthy Strangers   113

Chapter 12: Happy to Be Adopted   132

Chapter 13: The Hospital Connection   143

Chapter 14: Treated the Same   152

Chapter 15: An Exception to the Rule   161

Epilogue   175
Acknowledgements   179
References   181

Chapter 1

On Adoption: A Collective Memory

'To adopt a child is a great work of love. When it is done, much is given, but much is also received. It is a true exchange of gifts.'
—Pope John Paul II

Of adoptions and found families

We often assume, usually rightly, that couples would want to keep their own children. But this is not always possible. Many of us might know someone who is adopted or someone who has adopted. This is when a child is raised by a family or someone else with whom the adoptee might not have biological links. The phenomenon of being raised by someone other than the child's birth parents or a family not related to the child was not novel in Singapore's past. What was most distinct about these adoptions was that the children were 'given up' to couples who received them without these children being formally adopted, i.e., their transfers from one family to another were not accompanied by legal documentation. Such child 'adoptions' were common enough and most people of the older generation knew about these children. They were often given to Malay and Indian families, as well as Chinese, Eurasians, and even Europeans, Arabs, and Armenians, who took up residence in multiracial Singapore. The children given away were mostly Chinese girls.

The late 1920s to the early 1970s were difficult times in Singapore. Pre-independence Singapore saw a great deal of hardship and poverty. Some parents had little choice but to give away the children they had as they could not afford to take on another mouth to feed and another child to clothe. For the birth parents, having to feed one fewer child certainly reduced the burden on them: but this would not have been an easy decision for them to make.

It would be no exaggeration to say that children were given up to strangers: couples who were completely unknown to the birth parents of the child. The power of word of mouth was recorded in many of these cases of adoption. The adoptive parents would learn of the intent of the birth parents to give away the child through various means at their disposal such as recommendations of trusted relatives, friends, or even neighbours. And if strong ties were not established between the natural and adoptive parents at the onset of the transfer, the adopted child would grow up never knowing their birth parents, let alone the opportunity to meet them and build the relationship.

But there were also those who gave up their children to friends or neighbours who were willing to take in the child and raise them as their own. In these instances, the birth parents would have kept in touch with the adoptive parents, and links between the two families were maintained throughout the adopted child's life. Sometimes, however, the relationship might not have been strong enough, and, so, ties might have faded over time. For instance, if the friendship was not strong enough, sometimes the adoptive parents might have chosen to actively sever all ties for fear of losing the adopted child to their birth parents, especially when the child grew older and became suspicious that their adoptive parents may not be their 'real' parents at birth, after all. In this case, the adoption would be one of the most zealously kept secrets, leaving it to the child to create his or her reality.

Whatever the situation, trust was a necessary ingredient in these child transfers: the birth parents had a strong belief that the families taking in their children would take good care of them and not ill-treat them. In fact, in the eyes of the Chinese, the Indians and the Malays were seen as communities who cherished children. But rather than adopting a child through dependable individuals—whether relatives, friends, or neighbours—there were instances where religious institutions stepped in to 'facilitate' the transfer. If a couple wanted a child, the convent was the place to go. It played a crucial role in enabling couples to adopt a child through the orphanage the nuns ran at the Convent of the Holy Infant Jesus. Many of the older generation would remember the side gate of the convent, situated along Victoria Street, which bore the words: Gate of Hope. Babies wrapped in rags and newspapers who could not be raised by their own birth parents could be left at the gate, and the nuns would find homes for the children. But not all these babies who were dropped off were orphans. Some had parents who could not afford to raise them and had left the child at the gate, usually with a note describing how the family could not keep the child. Others would directly hand the child over to the nuns and were assured that they would find a loving home for the child.

These adoptive parents were magnanimous in every way. They had enormous levels of generosity and were willing to take on the children of others so that these children could grow up in a loving and caring environment. Living with these adoptive families into which the girls were transferred into gave them a new lease of life: their existence in many ways was much more comfortable than the conditions in which they might have grown up in, if they had stayed on with their birth parents. Their adoptive parents were not always well-to-do, but they gave everything that they could, within their means, to raise a child who was not their own. Especially amongst childless couples, they stood to gain from receiving the child. To them, adoption offered a path to parenthood. Other adoptive parents might have already had children of their own. But the extra child in the family gave them an opportunity to continue to build their families. Because they would have adopted a girl, they were sometimes more protective of the adopted child than they were of their own biological children. But for the most part, they never distinguished between the adopted child and their own.

To any child, the family is central in their lives, and this is no different for an adopted child. The child learns to become a member of a community. He or she grows up to be independent, learns how to live with others, adjusts in the community and becomes active contributors to society. In the case of an adopted child, the family into which the child has been adopted has a significant impact on their identity. The adopted child becomes, in every sense, a member of the family—he or she adopts the cultural values, ethnic traditions, and religious practices of the family as well as the language of the family. As young adults, these adoptees almost always ended up marrying someone from within the community, revealing how successfully these adoptees have become integrated into the family and the community of their adoptive parents. In these cross-cultural adoptions of Singapore's past, the Chinese girl adopted by an Indian couple often, as if quite naturally, transforms into an Indian girl through adopting the way of life of her adoptive parents. Likewise, the Chinese child who was adopted into a Malay family seamlessly integrated into the adoptive family and, in turn, the community of the adoptive parents.

On the part of these adopted children, the moment of epiphany would arrive when they would eventually learn that they were adopted, even if they had not been told about it by their adoptive parents. But for most of them, when the wheels of their adoption came off, they never saw their adoption as a crushing experience nor was discovering their adoption present itself as an earth-shattering event for them. This was because these children would have already suspected that they could be adopted given that they did not resemble any of their adoptive parents. Even if there was any slight suspicion that they could not be biologically related to their adoptive parents, they tended not to broach the subject with their adoptive parents for fear of hurting them. So, for many of them, it was business as usual after making this discovery. What was most important for them was that they took comfort in the overwhelming love, care, and affection that their adoptive parents had for them. Learning about their own adoption did not alter the relationship they had with their adoptive parents one bit. Hence the feeling of nonchalance would best describe their response to their adoption.

On the other end of the spectrum are those who found the discovery of their adoption traumatic, mentally, emotionally and psychologically. This was especially so amongst those who felt that they were deserving of being told the truth and relating it to a sense of fairness; only to realize that their adoptive parents had hidden the 'truth' of their adoption from them. The question of why they had not been told the truth haunted them for many years to come, with some even finding ways of seeking out their birth relatives, only to be disappointed in their quest.

For those who grew up knowing their birth families because their adoptive parents and birth parents kept close ties and the fact of their adoption was revealed to them—even at a fairly young age for some—their story would be the honourable exception. These adoptees would not only know that they were adopted but also the circumstances under which they were transferred and the reasons for being received into the lives of their adoptive parents.

Yet for all these adoptees, life is a journey of growth, remembrance, and realization. The anxiety they would undergo would be gradually replaced by a sea of calmness, and the confusion they would have encountered would eventually be engulfed by tranquillity because of the profound love they would encounter in the families into which they were adopted. Hence, the title of this book—*Little Drops*; deriving inspiration from the Tamil phrase '*siru tulli peru vellam*', meaning 'small drops make a great flood'. I have interpreted this as how the love showered upon the adopted child signifies one small drop of love at the onset of the bond, but over time, these tiny drops of love multiply, forming an ocean of love engulfing the child.

The reasons for writing this book

If not for the older generation of those residing in Singapore from the late 1920s to the early 1970s, the story of adoption amongst these individuals whose lives are documented in this book would not be known to many Singaporeans of the current generation. It is for this reason that this collection of biographies of fourteen adoptees was written. It traces and retells the reasons for which children were given away and why couples had chosen the path of adoption to build a family. More importantly, it focuses on what it means to be adopted as it uncovers the journey and lived experiences of these adopted individuals—their lives, experiences, and challenges. However, only what each adoptee wanted to share has been conveyed. Hence some stories might not be as seamless as one would expect them to be. Yet what is fascinating is that each of these biographies and the circumstances under which each person was adopted relates to a different facet of Singapore's history from the late 1920s to the early 1970s: the plight of individuals and their families; the strength of friendships and informal social networks; our migrant heritage; and the turmoil Singapore underwent during the Japanese occupation as well as the years leading up to the country's independence.

The adoptees, whose stories were selected for the book, do not speak with one voice. Their life histories reveal the rich fabric of Singapore during those times. Most importantly, as the collection of biographies reveals, their stories show how much can be learned from listening to them since each of the adoptees is a treasure trove of information on Singapore's past and the experience of being a transferred or adopted child. If not for the documentation of these stories, the phenomenon of child adoption, especially cross-cultural adoption, would slowly be forgotten in Singapore's history and fade away from the collective memory of Singaporeans.

Chapter 2

The Love of Children

Loving a child unconditionally

Raising and loving children is central to Malay culture. We often hear of parents overindulging their children: this, parents think, makes them happy, and their desire is to make the child happy too. Exercising the right to guide, nurture, and raise a child is considered to be a desirable task. The Malays, in particular, are known for their strong family bonds and typically develop a close relationship with their children. Children are also seen as precious and, thus, are treated with great care. How adults go about forging bonds with children show the love they have for children. All children should be showered with love, including those with any kind of disability. That is why Malays are more likely to receive children rather than give away children. Their love for children would only be bolstered by Islam, a religion which regarded children as gifts from God. Thus, when the possibility of receiving a child was presented to Aminah Hussein's adoptive parents, they could not decline the offer.

Tok Hussein and his wife, Siti, could not have children of their own. They had adopted a Malay child long before Aminah came along. She was a relative whom they took under their wing. But, alas, she passed on. Child transfers amongst relatives tended to be more common in the Malay community than one might think.

Usually, a couple who wants to give up a child, especially if they cannot afford to provide for the child, finds a wealthier relative to raise the child. Acquiring another child through adoption was the only option for the childless couple to fulfil their dream of starting a family. If a relative's child was not available, a Chinese girl or boy was welcomed.

Before Aminah, her adoptive parents did receive another Chinese girl. This was during the Japanese occupation. Sadly, the infant died from malnutrition. In a melancholic tone, Aminah mentions that if she had survived, she would have been around eighty today and that she, seventy-four years old now, would have had an older 'sister'.

Aminah's birth

Aminah was born in a private maternity clinic along Bencoolen Street in Singapore. It was December 1948, not long after the Second World War. Her birth, however, was only registered in January 1949 by her adoptive father. Her birth certificate contained her adoptive father's as well as his wife's personal details. There are countless reasons for which a couple would decide to give away a child. The inability to afford to provide for the child is one distinct factor. But Aminah was transferred not because her birth parents could not afford to keep her but because of an illness inflicted upon a family member at the same time her mother was carrying her. It was her biological father who had suddenly been taken ill during his wife's pregnancy. Fearing that the illness of her biological father might be an ominous sign linked to the child, a medium was consulted. The family was staunchly Taoist. Being recent immigrants from China, like many others in the late nineteenth and early twentieth century, it was not surprising that they clung on to their cultural beliefs tenaciously. They would zealously maintain their rituals, habits, and customs as they came to Singapore in search of a better life. In the case of a birth that coincides with the illness of a family member, it is not uncommon for the infant to be given away. After carefully scrutinizing the horoscopes of both her and her birth father, the news came from the medium. There was no other choice; Aminah had to be given away in order to preserve the life of her birth father. She was the third child in the family and the eldest daughter.

Aminah's transfer

Putting a child up for adoption is never an easy task, let alone the fact that it is heartbreaking. The welfare of the child is paramount in most cases. In fact, many couples who choose to give away their child would often seek out a family who could afford to provide materially for the child, aside from giving the child love and affection. But that was not the case with Aminah's adoptive parents. They were from a humble background. Her adoptive father was a driver, working in the same clinic as Aminah's biological father who was the pharmacist at the clinic. His wife, Siti, was mainly a homemaker although she did postpartum massages and occasionally prepared Malay *kuih* and curries to sell to their neighbours for a small income.

But what was distinct was that Aminah's adoptive parents were not strangers to her biological family. In fact, her biological father had known her adoptive father for some years already since they had been working together. So, when the devastating news came that the family would be better off giving away the child, it was only logical that Aminah's birth father turned to someone he knew—a longtime friend and colleague whom he could trust with his own child.

Giving away the child to a friend or colleague had its advantages: aside from knowing that his daughter would be loved and treasured, there is always the potential of being able to keep in touch with the child. That was exactly the case with Aminah.

A pact was drawn between her biological family and her adoptive father that would guarantee visits to the child every Chinese New Year. Aminah's father dutifully kept to his word: every Chinese New Year, he and his wife, together with Aminah, would pay visits to Aminah's biological family without fail. It was a gathering that would bring joy to her biological parents who always looked forward to seeing her.

Realization of her adoption

By the time Aminah was transferred, her adoptive mother was fifty years of age while her adoptive father was forty-two. This was her adoptive mother's second marriage while for her adoptive father, it was his first. Hence the possibility of having a child grew dimmer for the couple as the years passed. Thus, for Aminah's adoptive parents, Aminah was a blessing and the answer to their many prayers.

In the Malay community, older couples actually sought out transferred children, as did unmarried women, those who had late marriages or those who were divorced. Amongst older couples, however, the adopted child was seen as a beneficial companion to have around the house as their own grown-up children would have built their own families and moved away, thus spending less time with them. Fearing that their home might become an empty nest devoid of the love they kept alive with their own biological children, older Malay couples would reach out to relatives and ask if they would be willing to part with their children to be raised in another household, even if it is for a short while, as in the case of fostering. The same would go for adopting a child. Even receiving a child from outside the racial or kin group would never be seen as a problem. The child could be seamlessly assimilated into the Malay community by taking on a Malay name, speaking the Malay language, wearing the traditional Malay attire, and, most of all, becoming Muslim: hence the term *masuk Melayu* or 'entering Malaydom' to refer to the process of 'becoming Malay' and, in turn, becoming Muslim or *masuk Islam*.

But growing up, Aminah was completely aware of her Chinese roots. It was not only those visits to the home of her biological relatives that triggered her realization of her origins, but her biological mother never kept the adoption a secret. She would remind Aminah each time they met over Chinese New Year that she was her actual mother—'*saya lu punya mak*', which means 'I am your mother'—in her broken Malay. Aminah recalled she might have been in primary school then, but those words would stay in her mind.

Things were different with her adoptive mother. She would never ever utter a word about Aminah being an adopted child, to the point of even denying it on occasion. Implicitly, she could have felt insecure that her adoptive daughter might choose to return to her birth family if she found out the truth. Interestingly, her adoptive father displayed the same behaviour: he would never say a word about her adoption. This was only natural, especially since emotional bonds run deep after years of loving and caring for a child, even if the child is not one's own. Aminah's parents doted on her dearly, and the fact of her not being biologically related to them was never broached.

Schooldays

But blocking the truth of her adoption was difficult for another reason. Growing up, it became clear to Aminah that she was adopted. Her fair skin was an obvious giveaway. Her adoptive mother had the typical complexion of many from the Malay world. She could trace her ancestry to Java and like others from the region, she was 'brown-skinned', as they would be described. Her adoptive father was much darker in appearance and looked more Indian since he was of mixed parentage with an Indian father and a mother whose ancestors were Buginese, originally coming from South Sulewesi. In terms of her features, she did not resemble either of them. Aminah had fine Chinese features and wide cheekbones.

Although she was accepting of her own adoption, her classmates were less forgiving. Many taunted her for being an *anak angkat* or raised child. She was incessantly teased with the words '*kamu orang Cina*', meaning 'You are a Chinese'. In fact, nobody would believe her that her adoptive mother was her biological mother, especially since she was already fairly old when Aminah was in school. But Aminah was not alone. She had several 'Chinese' classmates who were adopted as well. They too suffered the same fate—the teasing about they 'being different' would never stop, however cruel it might have been, especially since they were children, an age at which they were vulnerable and needed to be protected.

Would her experiences have been different if she had gone to an English school? One would never know. For her primary school education, she attended Sekolah Melayu Siglap (Siglap Malay School) and was amongst the first batch of Malay students who graduated in 1960. On passing her examinations, she secured a place at Tun Sri Lanang Secondary School (Sekolah Menengah Tun Sri Lanang) but studied first at Tanjong Katong Girls' School from 1961 to 1962, pending the construction of the building of Tun Sri Lanang school in 1963. It was at the insistence of her adoptive parents that she found herself attending Malay schools; although Aminah herself secretly harboured intentions of attending an English school, seeing an English education as a channel of opening more doors for her if she wanted to work. However, she was only to find that her desire would be squashed. She implicitly knew that her adoptive parents would never allow her to attend an English school, fearing that she might convert to Christianity, lose her Malay values and *adat* (customs), and eventually choose to speak less Malay. For these reasons, they made the active choice on her behalf that a Malay school was where she would go. It was clear that the school she attended was important for them for one key reason: it was a powerful socialization agent, reinforcing her Malay values and identity throughout her formative years. Thus attending an English school was out of the question.

Foray into politics

During that time, Aminah's biological father entered politics, first as Chairman of the National Trades Union Congress (NTUC) and later as a Member of Parliament in the People's Action Party (PAP) from 1963 to 1984. This did not affect Aminah in anyway though. To her, her biological father was still her biological father. The only image she had of him imprinted on her mind was that of a loving and caring person.

Later, some years down the road, her own biological sister followed their biological father and entered politics. This was in 2001.

Her two families

As an adopted child, Aminah was immersed in a Malay environment—both at home and in school—and grew up into a fine 'Malay' woman. She learned about Malay culture, tradition, and social norms every step of the way, as if following a chartered course laid out by her adoptive parents. She also recalls enjoying attending religious school (*madrasah*) housed in a home in Jalan Hajijah, where she diligently set off to learn the Arabic language. Her adoptive parents' aim was that she would pick up the skills to read and write the Arabic language so that she could eventually read the Quran and pray in Arabic. Tok Hussein, his wife, and Aminah lived in a wooden house with an attap roof along Dunbar Walk. Their home was a safe haven for Aminah as she was a happy and contented child growing up.

Aminah's ties to her biological family continued to be strong since they were never severed in the first place. She would be in regular communication with her birth family as her biological mother would call her weekly to check on her, as if to look out for her well-being, even though she lived in another household.

Moving house

But links with her biological family were briefly cut when the Hussein family moved out of the area. Since the landlord had other plans for the land he owned, the family was forced to look for a new home. But while waiting for their new home, the family were forced to move several times, and, in the process, lost touch with Aminah's biological family.

Life went on for the Husseins. On one of their visits to Mak Chu's—Tok Hussein's sister—home in Sembawang, Aminah met the man she would eventually marry. As she entered the living room, she would pass a young Malay man who was on his way out of the house. She would later find out that he was working at a community centre nearby. But little did she know that he had taken a fancy to her although the encounter was brief. It was a few years later that he made known his desire to marry her to her parents. His name was Abdul Gapar, and he was a few years older than Aminah. To Aminah, Abdul appeared to be a good and responsible man with a stable job. Aminah had other suitors; she was highly sought after because of her fine features and light skin colouring. But her decision was final. On turning sixteen, Aminah became wedded to Abdul and had three beautiful girls in the years that followed.

Lost and then found

During the first few years of her marriage, there was no contact between Aminah's biological parents and her adoptive parents.

This spurred Aminah's biological relatives to be worried as to why they had not been contacted by Tok Hussein at all. The brief separation did not stop Aminah's biological parents from going in search of her and her adoptive family. Visiting Dunbar Walk one day, they inquired of neighbours as to Tok Hussein's whereabouts. Eventually, after several false leads, to their elation, they were able to locate Tok Hussein, his wife, and Aminah.

By then, Aminah had been happily married and was with child. As ties were rekindled, Aminah's biological parents were delighted for her, although her biological parents would have preferred if she had waited a year or two before plunging into marriage. But they were not entirely unhappy about her decision either. Her biological brothers made an effort to develop a friendship with Abdul over the years, even visiting the community centre where he worked since they too had jobs in government. They embraced him like a 'brother' in spite of their social differences—since Abdul was a Malay and they were Chinese. In fact, those differences around race, culture, and language seemed to diminish over time.

Until today, Aminah is in regular contact with her biological relatives in spite of the passing away of her biological parents, first her biological father in 2008, followed by her biological mother in 2022. They visit each other on birthdays and other celebrations. While she continues to visit the Chinese side of her family during Chinese New Year, they, in turn, visit her during the end of the celebration of the fast or Hari Raya Puasa as it is known in Malay.

Aminah counts herself to be massively blessed to know her biological relatives, unlike many adopted children who have lost contact with their birth family. To her, if she were ever asked by a stranger or an acquaintance if she was Chinese, Aminah had no problems revealing to them her Chinese origins. But she would always add a caveat: that she had been adopted into a Malay family. For her, the fact of being both Malay and Chinese posed no conflict. This is because Malay culture, unlike many others, seamlessly allows for an 'outsider' to be transformed into a member of the community not just through marriage, but through the process of receiving a child who is not related to them by birth and making him or her their own.

Chapter 3

Half-Eurasian

Love for children

Unlike children transferred into Indian and Chinese families, in the Malay community in Singapore and Malaysia, it is not unheard of for children to be transferred to extended kin, either through blood or affinal ties. For couples who could not have children of their own, what better way to acquire a child than through child transfer. Sometimes, a relative—especially an unmarried woman with no children—would take a keen interest in a child and end up raising the child with the permission of his or her biological parents. Thus, the term '*anak angkat*' or 'raised child' was coined. Conversely, it is not uncommon in the Malay community for a couple who is unable to provide financially for a child to give up the child to a wealthier relative. In this case, it is presumed that the person with greater economic means has the capacity to provide for the child. But exceptions did occur as in the case of Hazel (not her real name) whose adoptive parents were of modest means.

Her biological mother's side of the story

Born in 1971, Hazel was raised by an elderly couple who were relatives of her biological mother. The story goes that her biological mother had a daughter the year before. When Hazel came along, her biological mother felt that she could not cope with providing for another child. Hazel was told that she was given up for adoption when she was a few hours old, her mother begging her uncle—Hazel's granduncle—to take in her second daughter. Hazel was dropped off at her adoptive parents' home as soon as her biological mother had her.

Her adoptive parents' side of the story

The question of 'who am I as an adopted child?' has been asked by many adopted children. Hazel is no exception. In her case, the question was spurred by the discovery that her 'parents' were not her biological parents. Instead, they were her mother's uncle and his wife, respectively. The decision for them to receive Hazel was not an easy one. They had two other adopted children— one already married and one in his teens. So, initially they were reluctant to take her in for fear that they would not be able to provide adequately for her. Her adoptive father worked as a marine engine driver and was not financially well-off. Her adoptive mother, on the other hand, had stopped working and was a homemaker.

At that time, Hazel's adoptive parents were 'fairly old'. They were past their prime when Hazel came into their lives. This became an added burden on them since having sufficient resources was integral towards providing for a child. But Hazel's adoptive mother did not have the heart to send her away as soon as the baby arrived!

Realization of being adopted

Hazel recalls that her childhood days were simple. Although she was not raised in luxury, one thing was certain: her adoptive parents doted on her and saw to her every need as best as they could. They ensured that she was well-educated. Coming from a working-class background, she felt nothing but that depth of love her adoptive parents had for her in every effort they made to make her childhood a gratifying one. Her adoptive mother, in particular, was endlessly overprotective of Hazel. She was seldom allowed to go to the playground and stayed at home most of the time.

But growing up, she began to sense that her adoptive parents were not her 'real' parents. When she was eight years old, her teacher had asked for her guardian's signature. This had left Hazel wondering why her teacher had asked for her guardian's signature and not her parent's. Once home, she asked her adoptive mother if she had been adopted. However, her response was unexpected! From her countenance, it was clear that Hazel's adoptive mother was extremely upset with having been posed that question. That night, she overheard her adoptive mother arguing with her adoptive father, blaming him for not using his name as Hazel's father. Because of her adoptive mother's reaction, Hazel let the matter go, although her curiosity had been piqued.

Hazel also remembers making visits to the Social Welfare Department when she was growing up. There, the social worker would ask her if she was well-treated at home and if she faced any problems with her adoptive parents. At that point, she began to suspect that she was a fostered child. But every time the social worker inquired about the state of things at home, Hazel was quick to retort that she was adopted and not fostered. In her own words, 'the intent after all was to give away the child' and not to take the child back. In fact, in all respects, Hazel was a transferred child. Her adoptive parents had been acknowledged to be her custodians in the Certificate of Registration of Transferred Child document her adoptive father had signed in 1972.

Although her adoptive parents were absolutely silent on the matter of her adoption, hiding it from her for the most part of her childhood, she had a gut feeling that she was not the daughter of her adoptive parents. While she is unable to pinpoint the exact time when she had begun to realize this truth, she had in her possession her original birth certificate—the biggest giveaway, since it did not contain the names of her adoptive parents.

But it was in 1983, when the time had come for Hazel to get her identity card processed, that more of the truth began to be revealed. Although she had her birth certificate with her, her biological mother was summoned to school in order for Hazel to obtain her identity card. On looking back, however, Hazel was not too clear why her biological mother had to be present in school. But Hazel was unsure how to respond to her and felt embarrassed in the presence of her biological mother, since there was a lack of any emotional tie between them.

Relationship with biological mother and father

Oddly enough, as Hazel recalls, she had seen her biological mother at various relatives' weddings but did not know that she was her biological mother!

There were occasions when Hazel's biological mother would call. She would answer the phone and her biological mother would chat with her. However, most times, Hazel could sense from the facial expression of her adoptive mother that she did not like it when Hazel spoke with her biological mother, and, so, she kept the conversations short.

At the same time, she could not deny that the conversations were difficult since there was a lack of closeness between herself and her biological mother. This stemmed from the fact that she was not raised by her, let alone saw her on a regular basis. At times, she felt that the relationship was strained, especially when her biological mother would 'talk down' to her, comparing her with her biological sister, especially regarding their annual examination results. Moreover, the relationship lacked the love and affection expected from a mother to a daughter.

Ironically, Hazel ended up attending the same secondary school as her biological sister. She was a year older than Hazel. Whenever she saw her biological mother in school, Hazel deliberately avoided her, making a beeline in the opposite direction. She also did not join the co-curricular activity that she was interested in as her sister was in it. There was no attempt at all on Hazel's part to meet or speak with her mother and sister. After all, she felt that the relationship was marked by ambiguity.

As she became older—Hazel might have been around sixteen years old then— the opportunity to rekindle the relationship with her birth parents presented itself. And with this, she started to warm up to the fact of having two sets of parents. At that time, she thought this was a 'cool' idea. So, she began to visit her biological parents at their house, without the knowledge of her adoptive parents. She knew her adoptive mother would feel hurt. So, she kept those visits a secret. When Hazel started college, her adoptive father passed away unexpectedly. Given that her adoptive mother became a single, non-working woman overnight, Hazel approached her biological parents to ask for their financial assistance to help with her adoptive mother's expenses. But to her dismay, Hazel's biological mother refused to undertake any of the payments towards Hazel's education or upbringing. Naturally, Hazel was disappointed. Nonetheless, she continued to maintain a cordial relationship with her biological parents.

Fortunately, despite the financial difficulty faced by Hazel and her adoptive mother, the workman's compensation the family received following the demise of her adoptive father helped Hazel through her pre-university and university education.

Her relationship with her biological father, who was of Eurasian descent, was equally strained. When she needed him the most—to solemnize her marriage as required for Muslim marriages—he failed to turn up. Hazel had to postpone her solemnization and meet up with her biological parents to coax her biological father to attend. This incident hurt Hazel so much, more than being given away, that it caused the chasm in their relationship to widen further and ended in irreparable harm. In fact, at that time, her relationship with her biological mother fell apart to the point where it became irreconcilable. The day had come when the idea of having two sets of parents crumbled before her very eyes.

Relationship with extended biological relatives

Although her relationship with her own biological parents was neither strong nor a cordial or happy one, Hazel had an exceptional relationship with her biological uncle, her mother's youngest brother. Born on the same day, in the same house, and in the same year, her biological mother and her biological grandmother were destined to give birth on the same day. Hazel and her uncle share a special bond and close relationship. Till this day, they are in contact and keep up ties.

Being a Eurasian and a Malay all at once

As a married woman, Hazel continues to keep her maiden name as is the case with all Malay women. As she knew she has a Eurasian last name and at the same time wears a veil befitting of many Muslim women, this mismatch in her appearance and her race often draws the attention of colleagues and those who do not know her intimately. Very few are able to join the dots that she is of mixed descent, let alone an adopted child. In most cases, there is little incentive for her to explain things to outsiders.

Growing up in school, there was no question in her classmates' minds that Hazel was Malay. She spoke fluent Malay, and her everyday habits, by any measure, were that of a Malay. And as she proudly tells all her friends, *belacan* is a must in her daily fare. As a Malay/Muslim, she was also trained to fast during

Ramadan (the fasting month for Muslims) at a very young age, even if it was only for a few hours a day or a few days in a week or in a month.

While Hazel's relationship with her biological parents was not always amicable and they are now estranged, she openly acknowledges that, occasionally, she has had emotional struggles about her being given away. But as she became older, she gradually grew to be more open towards acknowledging the Eurasian side of her family. Now she embraces her Eurasian identity and would seize every opportunity to display her Eurasian heritage. For Hari Raya, sometimes she would include Eurasian dishes in the repertoire of foods served. One such notable dish is devil curry, a meat-based spicy curry made with candlenut, galangal (blue ginger), mustard seeds, and vinegar, from the Eurasian Kristang (Cristão) culinary tradition of Malacca, Malaysia. Occasionally, she would bake *sugee* cake, a dessert that is associated with Eurasians from Singapore and Malaysia. She also uses her Eurasian surname in her social media accounts.

Assertion of her Eurasian identity has not stopped there. Hazel has raised her son to acknowledge his Eurasian background. In her own words, 'I want my son to grow up knowing that being a quarter Eurasian is every part of his ethnic identity as much as being Javanese from his father's side.' Thus, rather than deny her Eurasian roots, she sees herself as a changed person in her adulthood: one who has come to accept and embrace her mixed heritage as well as her adoption.

To tell or not to tell

In many cases of adoption in Singapore's past, children grew up in homes in which they did not have biological ties with those providing them with care. However, the case of the Malays was an exception. Very often, the transferred child knew he or she was being raised in a relative's home and came to understand the reason why he or she was being raised by kin instead of his or her biological parent(s). There might be a few reasons for this unusual practice.

Explicitly telling the child about his or her parentage may be linked to the Islamic laws of inheritance: an adopted child does not automatically have a right to inheritance. In fact, Islam has strict inheritance laws spelling out how much an adopted child may receive unlike a birth or biological child. This does not mean that the adoptive parent cannot pass on a gift in the form of assets or money to the adopted child upon the adoptive parent's death. Under Syariah law, in his will, a Muslim man can only leave one-third of his estate to persons who are not legal beneficiaries.

But more importantly, telling the child he or she is a transferred child allows the child to freely interact with his or her biological family. In fact, there is no one right way to ensure that the child is placed in a good home, is raised well, and has all his or her needs taken care of. While being transferred to a wealthier relative was usually the norm if a child transfer occurred amongst relatives, this is not always the case, as we see from Hazel's experience. She was blessed to be raised by a couple who loved her dearly and who did everything to provide for her needs. And to this day, it is only for them that she has the deepest love and affection.

Chapter 4

Two Families to Call Home

Love for all things Indian

The curtains will soon be drawn open. Packery Thayyal gazed at her only daughter Jaiyanthi who was decked in a saree, ready for her next performance. Watching her daughter perform always made her heart swell with pride and joy. Growing up 'Indian' meant that she took delight in 'all things Indian', whether it was the *Bharatnatyam* dance tradition, Carnatic music, or the culinary culture. Her love for the Indian arts was something she shared with her husband, N. Sugumaran. Hence, when Jaiyanthi came along, it was no surprise that they were quick in cultivating in her a keen interest in dance. At the tender age of five, Jaiyanthi was off for her first classical Indian dance class.

It was Thayyal who shuttled Jaiyanthi to all her dance classes. Always clad in a *kurta*, unless she was attending an important function in which she adorned a silk saree, she would stand out in a crowd because of her Chinese features. Born as Sim Ah Moi and transferred to an Indian family as an infant, her story is intriguing. Her adoptive and biological mothers were no strangers to each other as they were neighbours in the same *kampong* and shared a deep friendship.

One child too many

As in many cases of child transfers from the 1920s to the late 1950s, couples had large families and Thayyal's biological parents had quite a brood. While there were maternity and child welfare centres including ante-natal centres in Singapore at the time, they only provided services for expectant mothers, nursing mothers, and young children but did not give advice on birth control. So, there was a lack of availability of contraceptives, which meant that couples could not plan their families. It was the norm that most women experienced multiple births. Some children survived while others, who were not so lucky, died of a range of diseases. With each birth, Thayyal's biological mother and father struggled, constantly wondering and worrying if they would be able to keep and feed the additional child who had come into their lives.

Meddling matriarch

However, little did her parents know that Thayyal's biological paternal grandmother was plotting to give her away as she was a 'tiger girl'. Tiger girls were, according to Chinese cultural beliefs, harbingers of bad luck. While her daughter-in-law was with child for the fifth time, she had no qualms about telling her Indian neighbour that she was hoping that the child was a boy and not a girl. These conversations would only ensue until the day Thayyal was born. On Thayyal's birth, the Indian neighbour assumed that her paternal grandmother was still interested in giving the newborn child away. Being interested in taking Thayyal in, the neighbour decided to approach the family. And to her delight, the child was a girl!

At the prodding of Thayyal's paternal grandmother, Thayyal's mother made the difficult decision to give her up. Initially, it was not her biological mother's decision to do so. Painful as it was, she acquiesced to her mother-in-law's demands and agreed to have Thayyal transferred—a fact that Thayyal would only learn in her adulthood.

But she was not the only child to be given away, as Thayyal and her biological family would much later come to know. There was another girl who was given away. In later years, conversations amongst the siblings revealed that she might have been handed over to the Convent orphanage. To this day, the family has no contact with that child, nor do they know her whereabouts.

Transferring a child can be an unsettling experience and did not always work out as well as it did in Thayyal's case. One of Thayyal's brothers, too, at a few days old, was forced to be given up to another family living in the same *kampong*. He was 'sold' for $800. But after a few days, on realizing that she had made a grave mistake, Thayyal's biological mother quickly returned the money to the couple who had received him and took him back. To this day he is called $800 in Hokkien, a nickname used amongst his closest of kin. With every fibre of her being, his mother vowed that she would never ever give away any of her children to another family from that day onwards.

This decision changed her son's fate forever. Unfortunately, she was powerless to do anything about her daughter who was given away and whose whereabouts are unknown to the family to this day. The only detail the family has is that she was a sickly child and that did not bode well for the family. Since at that time it was thought that it was inauspicious to keep a child who was constantly falling ill, she had to be given away.

Thayyal's transfer

When Thayyal was a few days old, her transfer to her adoptive parents was completed. On the day Thayyal was transferred, gifts were exchanged. According to Chinese custom, the transfer of the child was completed with the presentation of gifts of *angpow* (red packets of money), wine, chicken, and other delicacies and the like from the birth parents to the adoptive parents of the child. In the case of Thayyal, the gift comprised only clothing. Money did not figure in the transfer, possibly because Thayyal's biological mother and her adoptive parents were close friends.

In her teenage years, Thayyal observed that her biological mother and adoptive mother were more than just neighbours residing in the same *kampong* in Kolam Ayer. They were good friends. They interacted with each other regularly, a friendship that would continue to blossom over the decades even when both families moved to separate housing development estates in the mid-1950s when their *kampong* was earmarked for development to build schools, hospitals, roads, housing, and other public projects. Thayyal's adoptive parents, in contrast to her biological family, were fairly well-off and could adequately provide for her every need. They owned a brick house several blocks away from her biological family's home. Thayyal's adoptive mother herself and her husband had been childless for some years and often thought of adopting a child. On Thayyal's birth, it was no surprise that they were very pleased to welcome the child into their lives.

Giving up Thayyal to her adoptive mother was no less a difficult decision for her biological mother even though they both knew each other. For many years, she was severely troubled and filled with guilt for having given Thayyal away. But there was one consolation. She knew that Thayyal was in good hands, and she could visit her daughter whenever she wished. Such adoptions were commonplace because of how social relationships played out in the *kampong* setting of Singapore. People from the different ethnic communities interacted freely and many individuals and families developed deep bonds of friendships beyond their own racial group.

In those days, developing relationships of dependence were also not uncommon amongst people living in the *kampong*.

There was a strong sense of community and solidarity. When people struggled and faced different hardships, turning to neighbours for help was not unknown. At the same time, it was not uncommon for people to readily help each other in times of need. This also extended to helping care for each other's children, which in some cases led to child transfers.

Giving up a child to a non-Chinese family was not uncommon amongst Chinese couples. They knew that their child would never be sold into prostitution or any other vice—a persistent problem at that time, so much so that the colonial British government launched the Children and Young Persons Ordinance in 1948. In fact, during those times, there was a common perception of how the Chinese conceived of the girl child: she was a slave and could be easily disposed of and sold off to whosoever wanted her. That said, these child transfers which took place prior to the 1960s were usually not accompanied by any legal arrangements. They were common enough in those days because people had a deep sense of trust. Sometimes, even fictive kinships developed naturally, which in turn led to the transfer of children from one family to another.

As Thayyal looks back, she reveals how fortunate she was. Her adoptive parents were wonderful people and had taken great care of her. She had a happy and fulfilled childhood. They ensured she received an education and was treated royally. After all, her adoptive parents were childless and longed for a child of their own until Thayyal came along.

Her adoptive parents

Her adoptive parents were of Tamil and Telegu origin. Hailing from Thanjavur, Tamil Nadu, Thayyal's father was a *mandur* or a supervisor as well as a union leader for the Jalan Besar constituency during the British times. So, he was an eminent gentleman in the Indian community in Singapore. Aside from being known to be a kind and helpful man, he would open his home to others who had recently arrived in Singapore from India and provide them with money or lodging. At one time, the house they lived in was also used as a tuition centre for the children of newly arrived Indians. They could take up free English classes there so that the skill might open doors for them in the future in the working world. This was in stark contrast to the dwellings taken up by many of the immigrants arriving from India: they lived mostly in positively horrendous areas, consisting of attap-roofed houses with poor sanitation and a water source shared by several families.

Recalling her childhood, Thayyal remembers how her father, although a loving person, was strict as well. If she did anything wrong, he would sit her down and let her know why what she did was wrong and that her mistake should not be repeated. But it was he who ensured she acquired the finest clothing. Before Deepavali every year, he would bring her to Little India to a tailor to get her new outfits stitched. It was he who would buy Thayyal her first saree. She was eighteen years old when she donned the saree for the first time. As a child, she fondly recalls going to Bata—a shoe store—with him as an annual event. Come New Year before children returned to school, she always received a new pair of school shoes. He would also buy her the school textbooks she needed. At the Bata store, she recalls her father being very particular. When buying her shoes, he would ask her details like, 'Are the shoes too tight? Is there enough space in the toe area? If they are too tight, it is better we take a slightly bigger pair.' Hence shopping for new clothes and shoes meant that it was an outing with her father. It would also have been possible that he took an interest in clothing her because he controlled the purse strings in the family as was the case in most Indian homes, given the patriarchal structure of the family unit.

Thayyal says that the bond she shared with her adoptive father was especially strong. Her father's love for the Tamil language rubbed off on her. That in itself ensured that she received private tuition to learn the language in a proper and systematic manner.

To this day, she remembers her Tamil teacher Mr Murugaiyya, who taught her how to write the Tamil script. She believes her writing skills were honed at a very young age because of the tuition classes she took under him. Being fastidious paid off. For every lesson, she made it a point to turn up early so as not to be punished by him.

On the other hand, her adoptive mother, running a small eatery and a mama shop in the front yard of the family home, had a laxer attitude towards studies. She was a loving person, however, who took care of Thayyal's daily physical needs. She was a great cook as well! While Thayyal's father bought her clothes and shoes, it was her mother who dressed her up and would plait her hair in a style typical of all South Indian and Tamil girls.

Becoming aware of her adoption

Growing up, Thayyal knew for a long time that she had been adopted and her adoptive parents made no secret about this. As she recalls, she was very young, probably in primary school, when she was shown a photograph of a woman and told that she was her biological mother. At around the same age, the neighbours used to tell her that her biological parents were living in the same *kampong*, pointing in the direction of Block B. Curious, she would go around the other side of the neighbourhood and find her biological father plucking fruit from the guava tree. Often he would give her some fruits while she played with her friends. During Chinese New Year, her parents would come by faithfully every year with trays of Chinese *kueh* and cookies. Undoubtedly, Thayyal's parents took advantage of those visits to see how their daughter was doing. She would later find out that her biological father would cycle by to check if she was fine, sometimes inquiring of neighbours if Thayyal was well taken care of. Besides, she would often meet her biological parents in the neighbourhood, and they would be nice to her and would enquire if all was well with her.

Even at that young age, she had understood something was not quite right. Initially, Thayyal was extremely confused on seeing the photograph of her biological mother as she could not 'put two and two together', that the couple raising her were not her 'real' parents. At the same time, realizing that she did not bear a resemblance with her adoptive parents, she instinctively had a sense that she might have been adopted.

But as she grew older and more mature, her adoptive parents spoke openly to her about her adoption. They had shown her the documents of her legal adoption and her original birth certificate. By then, Thayyal had suspected her adoptive parents were not her 'real' parents. While she did go through a state of confusion initially, reality struck when her adoptive parents revealed the circumstances that led to her adoption, transforming rumours into truth.

As the years went by, she and her biological and adoptive families would gather regularly. It was then that she began to realize that the 'Chinese' family with whom her adoptive parents had actively interacted all these years were her biological relatives. Even her own biological siblings, whom she would play with in the *kampong*, would eventually be told that she was related to them by blood. While raised as an 'Indian' in every way, Thayyal's story is unusual in one significant respect: even as she grew up with her adoptive parents and engaged in Indian habits and customs, she was aware that she had a biological family which was Chinese—a fact that she was never shielded from.

Keeping in touch with her birth family

That her biological family kept in touch with her adoptive family warmed her heart. During the Lunar New Year, she looked forward to her biological mother visiting her with gifts in the form of food like chicken, duck, and all the Chinese *kuehs* (cakes). Her birth mother would often take the opportunity to tell her how much she wished for Thayyal to be 'back in her arms'. By then, Thayyal was aware that she had been adopted and took great pleasure in having two families to which she belonged. During Deepavali—the Hindu festival of lights—Thayyal and her adoptive parents would reciprocate by visiting her biological parents armed with a huge tray of Indian sweetmeats prepared by her adoptive mother. There was *murukku*—savoury, crunchy snack made from rice flour and *urad* dal flour, *laddu*— a sweetmeat made from chickpea flour, jaggery, and ghee or butter, and other treats which her adoptive mother would have spent days ahead of the festive season making.

These visits to her biological mother's home in the days leading up to Deepavali was an annual ritual until Thayyal's biological mother's passing in 2019 at the ripe old age of ninety-nine. As in family gatherings, all 150 members of the family turned up for her funeral, except for a handful of grand and great grandchildren who were residing abroad. Out of respect for her biological mother who was a Buddhist, Thayyal and her children dressed up in Chinese funeral garb and joined in the funeral procession to accompany the hearse to the cremation site. It was on such occasions that any outsider would have noticed the striking resemblance between Thayyal and members of her 'Chinese' family. That she was a 'carbon copy' of her siblings could not be denied. But when both her biological parents passed away, she participated in all the final rituals as a biological daughter would have. Her filial duty to her biological mother was expressed in another way. When her biological mother became ill in her old age, every child in the family did their part as a caregiver. This was no different for Thayyal, although she had been given away at birth.

Although feeling very much 'at home' with her biological family, because of cultural differences, Thayyal could only communicate with her birth parents in Malay as she only spoke Tamil and not Teochew or Hokkien. In those days, because of the merger of Singapore with Malaysia, Malay was the national language which she studied in school, although her second language was Tamil. She still remembers learning *peribahasa* or the Malay proverbs. Thankfully, communication with her siblings, who were closer to her age group, did not pose a problem. They were all fluent in English.

Unlike her biological family, which was considerably large because all her siblings were married and have children of their own and even grandchildren, her adoptive family was much smaller. Her adoptive mother was the only child who came to Singapore with her uncle from Andhra Pradesh in India as a young girl. Her adoptive father, however, had six siblings with whom he was very close. They were married and had children and grandchildren of their own. Bonds were close between Thayyal and her adoptive father's side of the family. To the present day, she speaks affectionately of her sisters-in-law. There was one sister-in-law in particular whom she was most fond of but, sadly now, has since passed away.

Having two families

In essence, Thayyal has had two families: a Chinese family with whom she shares blood ties and with whom she interacted regularly throughout the year as she grew up; and another into which she was transferred into, who cared for her daily well-being, and who would eventually see her married off. It was her adoptive parents who ensured she received an education, attending Sennett Estate Primary School and later Serangoon Garden Secondary School, where she attained her GCE O-Level. It was also her adoptive parents who would eventually gift her a terrace house located in Serangoon Garden Estate for her wedding.

She was only eighteen when she was married. The chosen groom was her adoptive father's cousin's son—a young, handsome man of twenty-three years. Thayyal and Sugumaran were no strangers to one another since they had grown up together and met each other regularly at family gatherings. It was Thayyal's father's brother who proposed the idea that Thayyal and Sugumaran tie the knot. Such marriage arrangements were not uncommon amongst transferred girls. Forging a marriage between the girl and a relative of her adoptive parents was seen as a way of sealing the incorporation of the 'outsider' Chinese girl into the Indian family.

Although the 'match' was arranged by her adoptive family, her biological relatives played a role in getting her married off. Thayyal's biological mother visited her before the wedding and presented her with a silk saree and some gold jewellery, signifying 'farewell gifts' as she married into and was received by another family. In Indian culture, gold jewellery is a choice gift for brides since the value of precious metals appreciated with time and could be exchanged for money, if the need arose. So it became a tradition to gift the bride with gold jewellery at a wedding. As amongst the Indians, it is also customary for the Chinese to present gold jewellery as part of the bridal trousseau. But it is the act of presenting a silk saree to Thayyal which was most revealing. It was an acknowledgement on the part of her own biological mother of Thayyal's Indian heritage and background. Her biological relatives were there for her throughout her major life events, including her engagement, followed by her marriage. Marrying in 1968, she would go on to have three children: two sons and a daughter.

If Thayyal is ever asked to identify herself, she almost always considers herself an 'Indian' woman. Whenever she meets her Indian friends, she naturally slips into speaking Tamil. Even after the passing of her biological mother, her own siblings have continued to acknowledge her Indian identity in many ways. When Jaiyanthi came of age, Thayyal's eldest brother presented her the prayer items needed for the puberty ceremony, although he himself was not Indian but Chinese. For Thayyal, every function or festival celebrated, every piece of news to be reported, and every incident which occurred would involve both her biological and adoptive families. For her, there was never any difference between her biological and adoptive families. In her mind, they seamlessly formed one huge, happy family.

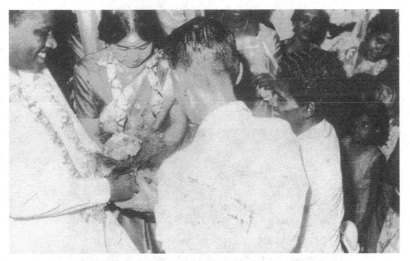

Thayyal's biological father and the uncle of Sugumaran, her husband-to-be, blessing the newlywed couple at the wedding ceremony. Sugumaran's father could not be present at the wedding as he was unwell.

Thayyal, her husband Sugumaran, and his two sisters.
On her lap is their first son, who had just turned one.

Family prayers at home to the deity Ganapati, whom devotees
pray to for prosperity and good life. Photo taken in 1990.

Chapter 5

What's in a Name?

A women's rights champion

Applause reverberated across the hotel ballroom as Anamah Tan slowly rose to her feet. Elegantly attired and with a broad smile on her face, she stepped on the stage to receive the award conferred on her for the many years of service she has tirelessly given to fight for women's rights in Singapore. Celebrated for her work as a family and human rights lawyer, Anamah earned for herself an illustrious legal career. Throughout her fifty-year-career as a lawyer, she was one of the greats championing against gender discrimination and domestic violence. A woman with a blend of grace, intelligence, courage, and grit, now her picture adorns the walls of the Singapore Women's Hall of Fame at the Singapore Council of Women's Organisations (SCWO) building along Waterloo Street in Singapore, joining other prominent and thoughtful women who have left an indelible mark on Singapore's social landscape.

However, Anamah's story was different to those of the many other women who became stalwarts in protecting and fighting for women's rights issues in Singapore. She was an adopted child of that period in Singapore's history during which children were given up across cultural groups to be raised in a family other than their own. As was common at that time among Chinese adoptee

children, instead of bearing a Chinese name to match her Chinese
appearance, she had an Indian first name bestowed on her by her
adoptive family.

Home background

Raised in a Ceylonese family, Anamah's adoptive father
Mr Nagalimgam was a law clerk in Donaldson and Burkinshaw.
An indomitable figure and a huge life force in her life, it was
her adoptive father who was significant in infuencing Anamah's
decision to study law as a young lady—initially, she had cherished
the idea of wanting to become a teacher. Her mother, on the other
hand, was a homemaker who raised five children of her own, four
boys and one girl, before Anamah came along. Hailing from one
of the many Indonesian islands, Anamah remembers her as an
elegant and beautiful woman, always clad in a *sarong kebaya*, the
batik long-skirt-like garment marked by motifs reminiscent of the
town of Solo in Java. Thus, it could be said that the family was of
mixed cultural heritage: with her father continuing to be Hindu
of Ceylonese descent while her mother was Indonesian Muslim.
She knows very little about how they had met, remarking that 'in
those days, children never asked such questions.'

Anamah's success in her adulthood might be attributed
largely to her happy, although strict, childhood. She attended
St Margaret's Girls' School where she excelled in her studies.

When she was first enrolled in that school, it was not called
St Margaret's Girls' School but the Church of England Zenanah
Christian Missionary School, otherwise known by its acronym
CEZMS, jokingly referred to as the Crocodile Elephant Zebra
Monkey School. Growing up was not all about school. On
occasions when she finished her homework on time, she was
allowed to amuse herself with the neighbourhood children.

One of her favourite things growing up was playing with
balloons. A vivid memory of her childhood was waiting patiently

for her adoptive mother to return from the horse races. In fact, as she looked back to her childhood as an adult, she is astonished as to how her father, who was a very conservative and serious gentleman, would be broadminded enough to allow his wife to go to the races. But that said, the races signalled a time of anticipation of joy for Anamah. She knew that her adoptive mother would return home with helium balloons. Anamah cherished those timeless moments of emotion. She was simply fascinated by these brightly-coloured balloons. The sight of them dancing in the air, defying gravity, elicited in her such joy.

As a child, Anamah also enjoyed attending weddings with her mother. She remembered having to sit with her legs tucked aside while her skirt or dress covered her legs. It was a difficult experience too, especially since one's legs could become numb after sitting in the same position for a few hours, let alone minutes. The most exciting part of attending weddings was that she looked forward to receiving the door gift at the end of the wedding ceremony.

Sadly, her adoptive mother passed on in 1951 when she was only eleven, leaving her only adoptive sister, who was many years older than her, to step into the shoes of their mother. Unlike her adoptive mother, her adoptive sister was a disciplinarian. She would ensure that Anamah completed her homework on time, and, if she did not or if she played too much, her adoptive sister would use the cane on her. If she tried dodging her adoptive sister's whips, the harder the blows she would have had to endure. That was when she learned that it was better to keep still and accept the punishment due to her. After all, she deserved it, especially if she had been naughty that day. In fact, Anamah would never dare bring home a report card with a red mark lest she incited the wrath of her adoptive sister. Even though she remembers those terrifying moments of her adoptive sister becoming angry with her, she is eternally grateful to her because, in every way, she ensured that Anamah would always be the best she could be. And without her, Anamah would not have achieved what she did later in life.

As for her adoptive father, she also remembers him to be a strict man and someone who was not exactly the kind of person anyone would want to joke with. Every evening at 7.00 p.m., she was expected to be seated at the main dining table with her books open, either studying or completing her homework—even if she was just pretending to keep busy. At 9.00 p.m. every evening, after spending the last two hours studying, Anamah would be sent off to bed.

It was also at 7.00 p.m. that her adoptive father would return home from the Ceylon Sports Club, where he met friends, although he himself did not drink, smoke, or gamble. It was also at this time that he would have dinner by himself, probably preferring to be alone since he was vegetarian while the rest of the family ate meat. And if he did not see Anamah at the table with her books, this would have incurred his wrath as he would have been expecting her to be reviewing her homework by this time. But he never raised his hands to her, as far as she could remember—not even once. He did have a few walking sticks though which he used in place of a cane, but they were only reserved for her adoptive brothers, if they had stepped out of line and engaged in any transgressions.

Anamah's adoptive father was fairly well-to-do, although he would later fall on hard times. The family had an old servant who came from China and was with the family until Mr Nagalingam passed away. She was like a family member and took great care of the children.

Her biological father

Although she was an adopted child, that fact never crossed Anamah's mind. For one, she was often told that she looked like her adoptive mother, who was fair-complexioned. But growing up, she could recall the regular visitations of a gentleman dressed in a suit (and mind you, not many men in those days wore suits!). She remembers this man to be fairly tall, although, in hindsight, nearly every adult would have been tall to a child. She might have been about five to six years old at that time. Whenever he came by to visit, Anamah's adoptive mother and sister would end up conversing with him while Anamah was told to go off to her room. This was common in those days. 'We did not sit around with the visitors as children were seen and not heard.' Although she did not know who he was, she was always excited to see him since his visits meant that she would receive a little red packet of money from him. Even though it would have been a paltry sum at that time, any small amount of money made her heart flutter with excitement.

But little did she know that the gentleman would turn out to be her biological father. She would learn this later, in her adulthood. Of the little divulged to her, she was to learn that her biological father had two wives. This was not uncommon in those days as being able to afford more than one wife signified one's standing in society.

Being the only daughter of the second wife, Anamah was transferred as a baby to Mr and Mrs Nagalingam in 1940—just before the Japanese Occupation—while her biological father and his wife kept her two brothers—their two sons. She would later learn that her father had also given away another daughter from his first wife to a Chinese farming family, a family that lived half a mile from the road where she lived with her adoptive family, in another *kampong* along King's Road. As Anamah was growing up, she had learned about the existence of this biological sister by sheer accident. One day while playing with the neighbourhood children, someone pointed out to her a young girl on a bicycle racing down the road. 'Look, that's your sister!' Entirely consistent with her middle-class upbringing as she lived in a bungalow along King's Road perched on top of the road, Anamah quickly retorted, 'How can she be my sister? She's so dirty and scruffy!' She found their claims to be patently false and quickly erected an arbitrary wall between herself and her supposedly biological sister. It turns out that these were the exact group of children who would relentlessly attack her by teasing her about her being an adopted child. As she never thought of herself as being adopted, she would in turn get into fist fights with these children, declaring, 'I am Ceylonese and not Chinese.' In every one of those 'fights', Anamah would bludgeon them with this same point repeatedly until she had the last word.

Realization of her adoption

But little did she realize the truth, at least at that time. It was only when her adoptive mother passed away that the unimaginable occurred. As she helped her adoptive sister, Zaleha, to clear her mother's belongings, Anamah discovered amongst the papers a letter from her biological father to her adoptive father: 'I am giving you my daughter and I hope she will grow up to be a filial and obedient daughter to you.' Given her intellect, Anamah swiftly deciphered the truth—not only was she adopted, but the letter had disclosed her Chinese name, thus revealing her true identity!

While for others such a discovery might have been too difficult to accept, for Anamah, life continued as usual. She went to school, received her pocket money, finished her homework, and got her usual caning if she did not finish her homework on time. That her adoptive parents and siblings were not related to her did not matter to her one bit, nor was she moved to go in search of her biological relatives. For her, her adoptive parents were the only parents she ever had and she never saw them in any other light. In fact, Anamah fondly recalls how they doted on her and showered her with immense love and affection, especially since she was the youngest child in the family. There was never even an occasion when she was treated any differently from her adoptive siblings. In fact, when it came to the division of the estate upon her adoptive father's death, he had left each of his biological children as well as Anamah an equal share. So, there was no distinction whatsoever between his own biological children and Anamah. If anything, Anamah was spoilt rotten by her adoptive parents. She had all sorts of toys and anything she wanted within reason.

While she felt no motive to go in search of her biological relatives, it was years later in her adulthood that she came to know the purpose for which she had been adopted: her adoptive mother had wanted to have one more girl but was unable to conceive. Having heard that a Chinese gentleman living in a *kampong* not far from their own home along Farrer Road was giving away his daughter, Anamah's adoptive parents decided to take her in.

Also, it was in her adult years that she would discover her own biological brothers. Growing up, she often wondered who the young Chinese boy was who would come to their house to pick up books her adoptive brothers had used the previous year. She learned that the Chinese boy was none other than her own biological brother who was quite happy with inheriting second-hand books from Anamah's adoptive brothers who did not need them anymore. It was with this brother, who was older than her, that she later developed a very deep bond after he had sought her out. Although she had the chance to meet her own biological mother later in life, their relationship was never close. 'It's the fact of proximity . . . You don't see and live with them, so the emotional closeness is not there.'

To law school

On passing the Senior Cambridge exams—that is what GCE O-Level was called in her days—Anamah applied to the Teacher's Training College to fulfil her dream of becoming a teacher. After a series of interviews, she was admitted to the college. But her father would not have any of that. He called the principal of the college and told him that his daughter was retracting her application and that she was going to go to the university instead to study law. He never considered what Anamah might want to do with her life. However today, she is grateful for the far-sightedness of her father and his absolute authority over her educational choices and career path. This was the start of her journey as a legal practitioner.

It was in 1959 that she entered the Law Department at the then University of Malaya. For the most part, law school was a great deal of hard work, and Anamah could never dream of letting her adoptive father down. Anamah's adoptive sister Zaleha played a pivotal role in ensuring her success. Because Anamah had to rote learn many cases, her adoptive sister helped by making written copies of law case notes on her behalf. Each day, she travelled to and fro from her home to the Bukit Timah campus. Although she would have liked to stay on campus like many other students did, it would have never been possible given her strict upbringing.

One of the most vivid recollections she had of her first year of studying law was the Freshies Orientation Ball. Anamah was the only student who did not sign up for the ball, to the surprise of Professor Sheridan, the first Dean of the Faculty of Law at the University of Malaya, who had expected that every student attend. She knew her adoptive father would forbid her attending. After all, he was not one who would allow her or her adoptive sister to date any man, let alone go out partying at night. In fact, he was strict to the point where boyfriends were an absolute no-no and Anamah would never dream of going against his wishes.

When queried by Professor Sheridan, Anamah candidly told him that her father was not the kind of man who would approve of her attending the ball. Refusing to accept a no for an answer, Professor Sheridan asked to see Anamah's adoptive father.

The date was set. Professor Sheridan appeared at the family home. Retreating into the kitchen to prepare tea for their guest, Anamah quietly left the living room when Professor Sheridan started to talk to her adoptive father. To her surprise, after the visit, Professor Sheridan managed to convince Anamah's adoptive father to let her attend the ball. Her adoptive father agreed to acquiesce only if Professor Sheridan could get her a reliable chaperone. He would pick her up at an appointed time and bring her back at the stroke of midnight and not a minute later.

Her dream had come true. She was going to attend the ball against all odds. Anamah thoroughly enjoyed the evening. She danced the cha-cha—which she had been secretly practising for many years without the knowledge of her adoptive father—with her classmates, whether male or female, to rock & roll numbers. To her delight, she also won the 'best dressed' competition that evening!

Becoming a lawyer

Finally, in 1963, Anamah graduated from law school. She was one of three women admitted to the bar in that same year. Accepting the advice of Edward Anselm Parker under whom she did her pupillage at Donaldson and Burkinshaw, she chose not to pursue a career in litigation. Instead, her first job was in the Housing and Development Board (HDB) as an assistant estate officer, the first woman so employed to see if the job was suitable for a female. Although she did not utilize her legal training directly as she worked in the estates' office, her law studies did prove helpful, especially when she had to work on tenancy issues and the sale of flats.

Several years later when she turned thirty, Anamah decided to seize the opportunity to work first as a Junior Partner in Leicester and Chen and thereafter as a legal assistant in Tan, Rajah and Cheah, doing mainly litigation and conveyancing. After her return from the United Kingdom, where she was admitted as a solicitor in England and Wales, in 1984 she decided to start her very own law firm, Ann Tan and Associates, with the blessings of her husband. She experienced instant success after a year. Clients came to her via word of mouth (as no advertisements or even calling cards were allowed by the legal profession then) and her reputation as a family lawyer gained momentum.

Family law was second nature to Anamah. She always thought women had the 'short end of the stick', and, so, going into family law was the most logical path to take. Since then, she has never looked back.

Heart for serving others

As her legal career took off, she became well-known in the women's rights circles in Singapore. She first started off as a founding member of the Singapore Association of Women Lawyers (SAWL) in 1974 and later as a founding member of the Singapore Council for Women's Organisations (SCWO). She was its president from 1991 to 2000. In that capacity, she played an instrumental role in raising funds for its new building on Waterloo Street. Later, between 2003 and 2009, she became president of the International Council of Women. Her work in the public domain did not stop there. A few years later, she was credited with having established the Singapore Association of Women Lawyers (SAWL) for the purposes of engaging in pro-bono work for disenfranchised women in Singapore and to remedy the many injustices these women faced. Then, in 2004, she became the first Singaporean female to be elected as a member of the United Nations' Committee on the Elimination of Discrimination against Women (CEDAW).

Serving others came naturally to Anamah as she had opportunities to reach out to others while she was growing up. In fact, her passion for volunteer work started when she was a young girl of twelve in St Margaret's Girls' School. She recalls the time when she served in a joint school project together with their brother school—St Andrews School. Together with their teachers, groups of students would run a clinic in the *kampong* in the Potong Pasir area every Monday. With empathy, she describes the villagers and how they were very poor and lived in such dilapidated conditions. There was no doctor and so they looked forward to the medical team from the school visiting them to help clean their wounds. Anamah also vividly remembers that there was no electricity in the village except for one power source which came from the largest house located at the centre of the village. It was the centre of activity for the village. The house looked like a huge stage raised above the ground on stilts. From that one source, water was boiled to sterilize the medical equipment that was used to clean the wounds of the villagers. It was difficult work, she recalls. Moreover, because the *kampong* did not have paved streets, it took walking for around a mile to get to the village. There were pig and chicken faeces everywhere! So, they had to watch where they were going, especially when it poured.

Another reason that paved the way for her to develop an empathy for the less fortunate was a family she had helped out when she was a young officer working in HDB. She remembers an Indian lady who had a string of children but was unable to pay her rent. This was not because her husband could not afford paying the rent of their flat but because he fell into a bad habit of spending his monthly wages on drinks whenever he received his pay cheque.

Thankfully, the *toddy* shop which he would frequent finally shut down. Till today, she remembers how, as an officer, she was able to help the family and see the positive impact her help had on them. Having to evict them would have been too painful to bear.

Her name and her appearance

For the longest time, Anamah went by the name Anamah Nagalingam. This was before she was married. At that time, she often donned a saree when she attended public events, causing a look of consternation from those around her who could not fathom why a Chinese-looking woman not only bore an Indian name but was also wearing an Indian costume, namely the saree. As they struggled to put two and two together, cheeky Anamah enjoyed watching the reaction of others around her. 'The situation posed a wonderful feeling . . . that you have an advantage over others because they find themselves not being able to clearly express what's on their mind!' All this was because of the mismatch between her name and her physical appearance.

As in many societies, in Singapore people often carry names that are consistent with their own ethnic identity. A Chinese had a Chinese name or a Western first name and a Chinese last name while an Indian would have an Indian first name and an Indian last name, with the exception of Indian Christians who might have Western or Christian first and last names. In this respect, Anamah was the exception. Throughout much of her career as a lawyer, she had an Indian first name and a Chinese last name, thus turning heads amongst people who did not know her background.

But, as the years went by, Anamah married and took on her husband's last name—Tan. It was also at this time that she chose instead to wear more Western clothing as it was too inconvenient to tie a saree, especially when she did not have the luxury of time to get dressed in the morning. To some extent, this put to rest some of the confusion people had about her racial background.

But amongst those who would meet her for the first time in her professional circles, there was still the puzzling question of how she became known as Anamah, which is a quintessentially Indian woman's first name. But since she was a known figure in the Singapore community and her story of adoption became increasingly known to some, people began to understand a little more about such cross-cultural adoptions, which were not uncommon during pre-independence Singapore.

Chapter 6

The Intermediary

The role of a 'go-between'

After trying unsuccessfully for a child, many couples often turn to adoption to fulfil their desire of having a child. Child adoption can be a difficult process since the couple would need to identify a family that might be looking to give up their child. In many instances, an adoption agency is approached through which an interested couple is connected with a child whose biological parent(s) have decided not to raise the child themselves for various reasons. In the past, in Singapore, adoption brokers or a go-between played a similar role of being a mediatory point in connecting people. Sometimes, the person received a handsome fee, depending on whether the family was wealthy and could afford the services of the broker or go-between.

Such was the case of Evangeline Sim. The mediator involved did not receive a fee and saw her task as an act of kindness, connecting Evangeline's biological parents with her adoptive parents. Growing up, Evangeline called this woman 'Aunty' unaware of the role she played in her adoption. She was a tall, slim woman of considerable influence and many around her seemed to respect her. Little did Evangeline know that it was this woman who had introduced her biological parents to her adoptive parents, thus leading to Evangeline's transfer.

As with many adopted children of her generation in Singapore, Evangeline was never told during her formative years she was adopted. There was nothing to lead her to believe that she was not biologically related to the family who raised her. Even her physical features resembled those of her adoptive parents, although they belonged to the Teochew dialect group, while she was Cantonese by birth. Despite these similarities, the unavoidable discovery of being adopted was a highly emotional experience for Evangeline, just as it was for many other adopted children.

Discovering the truth

The truth bomb was dropped when the time came for her to make her Identity Card or IC. She was twelve years old at that time and needed to produce documentation of her birth in order to 'make' her IC. Receiving her birth certificate from her parents, she was astounded to discover that the document did not bear her adoptive mother's name. Instead, in that column was the name of a woman she did not know. There could not have been a mistake since Evangeline's Chinese name Quek Siew Yong appeared in the document. When she asked her adoptive mother, she was simply brushed aside and told, 'In those days, people make errors and mistakenly put someone else's name down as your mother in your BC.' Evangeline's heart, however, grew severely troubled by that one incident, only to realize later that the unsettling feeling she had would only fester throughout her teenage years, never to go away.

As the years passed, in the hope that the truth might be revealed to her, Evangeline decided she would ask her adoptive father the same question she posed her adoptive mother at the tender age of twelve: 'Why is there another woman's name on my birth certificate?' This time the reply she got from her adoptive father was even more astonishing. He explained he had an affair with another woman and her name had to appear on Evangeline's birth certificate! He then went on to explain that the woman did not want to have anything to do with him or Evangeline, and hence she 'ran away', leaving Evangeline in the care of her father. Because his own wife was forgiving of the transgression he had made, Evangeline's adoptive father explained, she allowed him to take Evangeline into their family and raise her as their own. But that story too did not sit well with her as it sounded incredible, and she knew it was meant to steer her away from seeking the truth. That gnawing feeling never seemed to leave her.

Days of her youth

For most of her teenage years, Evangeline would describe herself as a 'troubled child' because she had so many unanswered questions about who she was and who her real parents were. For her, 'life was not right without learning the inescapable truth' about her adoption and the result for her was numerous disturbed episodes she would go through. Although her adoptive parents were Christian and the family went to church regularly on Sundays, as a teenager, Evangeline stopped going to church as she found it meaningless. Questions around her adoption affected her behaviour in other ways. In school, she often played truant as a sense of emptiness set in, and she was preoccupied with wanting to know her roots. She felt an increasing sense of emotional separation from the couple who had adopted her. She could fathom the possibility that she might have been adopted. Her suspicion of being an adopted child had been aroused by the fact that she was treated differently from her 'sister' by her adoptive parents. They constantly showed favouritism towards her only 'sister' who was twelve years older than her: it seemed like her 'sister' always ate first, was bought the nicest of clothes, and was showered with all sorts of gifts. Things did not feel right, and true enough, her suspicions were confirmed soon after becoming a mother.

Evangeline wanted to leave home as soon as she could, and marriage seemed to provide that convenient excuse. In 1974, at the young age of seventeen, she ended up tying the knot with a man who was a drummer in a band called 'Traffic Jam'. She used to frequent music joints as a pastime, leading to their encounter. The story of Evangeline's discovery of her adoption was almost melodramatic. It happened when she was nineteen. It was after about a year of having her first child. She was about to leave her home for her adoptive parent's home when a phone call came. It was Aunty at the other end of the phone, telling her that her biological father had passed on. She was confused initially and thought it was ridiculous given that her 'father'—she assumed Aunty was talking about her adoptive father—was still alive and kicking and waiting to see his grandchild that afternoon. But then the rude shock came. She was told that her adoptive father was not her 'real' father and that her 'actual' biological father had passed away. It was then that the realization of her adoption sank in. Although the truth was painful and shocking, it seemed like 'the pressure valve was released at last'.

The wake

But little did she expect to be summoned to attend the wake of her biological father that day. Initially, she was reluctant to attend because she did not know the man! However, the day after learning the news of his passing on, Evangeline had a change of heart. Aunty also urged her to attend the wake, explaining that it was her biological father's last wish before his death to see her, mumbling something to the effect that 'if he didn't see her, his ghost would come and look out for her.' Unfortunately, his wish was not realized as he passed on before he could meet Evangeline face-to-face.

At the wake, once again she chanced to meet Aunty. It was also at the wake that Evangeline discovered one crucial fact: that Aunty had played the role of mediator between her biological parents and her adoptive parents. It was she who was instrumental in getting Evangeline transferred from her biological parents to her adoptive parents. It was in 1956. The minute Evangeline was born at the Kandang Kerbau Hospital, she was handed over to her adoptive father by her biological father. Instead of her biological father, her adoptive father went to register the birth, thus explaining how his name ended up appearing in Evangeline's birth certificate. On the other hand, it was impossible to fake her biological mother's name, and, so, her biological mother's name appears in her birth certificate.

Before Evangeline was transferred to her adoptive parents, a pact was made between Aunty and Evangeline's biological parents: 'this child should never be told that she was adopted.' Similarly, Aunty persuaded Evangeline's adoptive parents to take an oath to never breathe a word to the child about her adoption. Thus, Evangeline's adoption was kept concealed from her 'like a secret', and the story of her adoption was concealed as she was growing up. At the wake, she was to make another discovery: Aunty was the sister of her adoptive father and she was good friends with Evangeline's biological relatives. Hence, she was the go-between who eventually brought the two families together, leading to Evangeline's adoption. But the families never kept in touch actively with each other after Evangeline was transferred. For Evangeline, the pieces of the puzzle began to fall into place.

But there was an additional detail to her story that also emerged, as if the 'secret' story of her adoption was rearing its head all at once after years of being suppressed. She found out the reason why she was given away from 'a couple' who were also present at the wake. In fact, the couple was familiar with Evangeline as every first day of Chinese New Year, she would meet them at Aunty's home together with her adoptive parents.

Those gatherings were deliberately orchestrated from the day Evangeline was transferred to her adoptive parents. One of the demands to which Evangeline's adoptive parents had agreed to was that they would ensure that this 'couple' would get 'to see' Evangeline every year. It turned out that this couple was actually Evangeline's oldest biological brother and his wife. It was also at the wake that they provided a crucial link to the story of her adoption.

What had occurred was this: Evangeline's biological mother and her eldest son's wife happened to be pregnant at the same time. Evangeline was born on 29 September and her nephew on 1 October. It was deemed to be an embarrassment or *paiseh* according to Chinese custom for a woman in her forties to be pregnant at the same time as a relative of the younger generation—such as a daughter or a daughter-in-law—who was in her twenties. Hence, her biological mother decided it was best to give Evangeline up for adoption. That way, she could enjoy being a grandmother and help look after her first grandson. She had to make a choice between keeping her youngest child and her grandson, and she chose the latter.

Although Evangeline's biological mother was not a woman of malicious intent, her decision could be read as a heartless and selfish move since she was swayed by the concern of 'saving face', giving away her own biological child. There was nothing to defer, deflect, or derail her plans. The family was of modest means, which could have been a reason for the decision to give Evangeline up. Residing in a *kampong* in Katong, the family would have struggled to provide for another child in the same household. This provided the additional 'push' for her biological family to give Evangeline away.

Coping with the pain of her reality

Although feeling that the answers to her questions had been finally revealed to her, Evangeline was left distressed. She felt 'unwanted' and 'like she was a mistake' in the lives of her biological parents. At that time, she was very upset to find out about her adoption in spite of already leading a life of her own: having newly married and starting a family. On looking back, she attributes her 'healing' from the trauma she experienced to the critical role played by her husband, Gordon. He was the 'meteor in her life'. It was through him that she learned that she needed to move on in life and that she did not need her biological relatives. Going forward, her transformed life would bear his fingerprints. She was also very young and possibly, as she explains later, immature and did not know how to deal with the raging emotions resulting from learning about her adoption.

Both she and her husband adopted Christianity in their twenties, although her first brush with Christianity was much earlier, given she had been adopted into a Christian family. Aside from her husband, Evangeline acknowledges that her faith in Christ has also been critical in helping her heal from the pain of her adoption, citing that 'God has a wonderful plan for each one of us' and 'to God be the glory in all things in life'. In fact, it was through the church—she, her husband, and their family all attend—that she received her baptismal name Evangeline.

Contact with her biological and adoptive relatives later in life

Over time, there were several attempts on Evangeline's part to contact her biological relatives, especially as she became older and more mature, and her own children were adults. After the death of her biological parents, there were many occasions when she would be invited to the homes of her biological siblings to celebrate birthdays, baby showers, and other events. But because her husband came from a very large extended family and had ten siblings himself, she did not feel compelled to go and constantly seek out her own biological relatives. So, Chinese New Year meant that she would spend time with Gordon's family and not hers. Whenever all his relatives gathered, there would be more than a hundred of them, including children, nieces and nephews, and grandchildren. Her relationship with her husband's relatives could be described as very close as they meet very often and keep in touch regularly. In Gordon's own extended family, there are several adoptions. Amongst them is his own older biological sister who was given away to an Indian childless couple at birth. She always kept in touch with her biological family. So, Evangeline did not feel like an 'outcaste' for being an adopted child. She felt very much at home since her identity of being an adopted child was something she shared with several members of Gordon's immediate family.

Her relationship with her adoptive family was more complicated, however, since her experiences of growing up with them were tempered by mixed feelings. For the most part, she had a fairly close relationship with them. She also learned later in adulthood about how her adoptive parents struggled financially to look after two children, which helped Evangeline put in perspective why she might have been treated differently from her 'sister'. At the time, her adoptive father was working as a clerk in the Singapore University while her adoptive mother was a homemaker. That they might have been 'forced' to take Evangeline into their lives against their wishes could also have explained the unequal treatment she felt she had received growing up. But at the same time, Evangeline expressed her gratitude towards her adoptive parents. They provided her with 'a roof over her head', fed her, clothed her, and gave her an education. To this day, Evangeline recounts that having been adopted by them was one of the most important experiences she had since she was introduced to Christianity, and has come to deeply understand that 'all things work together for good to those who love Him'. Although she felt the hurt by being treated differently from her adoptive sister, the relationship she had with her adoptive mother healed over time, leading Evangeline to be the daughter who ended up caring for her adoptive mother in her old age. Because her adoptive mother was from China, she did not have an extended family in Singapore and was wholly dependent on Evangeline as she grew old. As for her adoptive father's relatives, Evangeline has kept in touch with a few of them, including Aunty who was responsible for overseeing her adoption. After the passing away of her adoptive parents, she has had little, if any, communication with her adoptive sister. This is not surprising, especially since Evangeline said pointedly, 'She never accepted me nor treated me well.' However, she has been in touch with her adoptive sister's two sons. Evangeline affectionately calls them her 'nephews' and enquires about her adoptive sister's well-being through them.

In her adulthood

Although as a young woman Evangeline was reluctant to talk about her adoption with her friends or her classmates, later in life, Evangeline accepted her adoption fearlessly. She now speaks about her adoption openly, probably because she has matured in her thinking over the decades, gradually accepting the fact of her adoption. Even her adoption story has had a positive influence on her own children. One of her daughters herself has adopted two beautiful brothers as infants through the Social Welfare Department in Hong Kong—not any individual broker or go-between, as occurred in Evangeline's case—when she and her husband worked in the city for several years. Before she and her husband made the decision to adopt, they first consulted Evangeline and her husband. While Gordon advised that they have their own children, Evangeline was happy that her daughter desired to give a child a loving home instead of having her own children. But her only advice was that they never hide the fact of their adoption from the two boys.

Feeling that her mother knew best in these matters because of her own adoption experience, Evangeline's daughter understood the importance of revealing her sons' adoption story to them so that they would never feel that the fact of their adoption was hidden from them. To help her in this endeavour, Evangeline's daughter started to buy books on how to explain adoption to her adopted children. Aimed at helping adoptees walk through their adoption experience, she felt that these books would open up a journey through which her sons would understand their own adoption. For her, Evangeline's counsel made the most sense since it actively encourages an attempt to understand the adopted child's perspective in the adoption conversation. It was also the most empathetic thing to do: to tell the child that their own biological parents or family members were unable to take care of them but there were caring individuals—not related to them— who stepped into the shoes of their biological parents. They were there to provide a 'forever family' and a loving home to the child. According to Evangeline, the act of concealing the child's adoption is unacceptable, even if the intention was to protect the child from any form of hurt. Instead, conveying the truth to the adopted child in a spirit of love and affection should be seen as the best way to help the child in understanding his or her roots.

Chapter 7

The Indian Sister

Childhood days

Thangah Koh's childhood was immensely happy. In the *kampong* in Aljunied, called Lorong Sungkai, where she grew up, she would play every day with her 'best friend', Fatimah. Common games they played were 'hop-scotch' (a game in which players hop over a series of squares drawn on the ground), 'five stones' (in which stones are thrown in the air and caught by the players, testing their skills at not dropping a stone), 'zero point' (the rubber band jumping game), and 'tin-can telephone' (in which a string connects two empty milk tins through which two people ingeniously talk to each other). Every day after the school bell rang, Thangah remembers how she would rush home to meet Fatimah so that they could play. Their friendship was so deep that they spent a great deal of time together, including the evening *Mahgrib* prayers when Thangah would join Fatimah in the daily *mengaji* or Quran recital. Little did she know that Fatimah was actually her biological sister, even though they bore a slight resemblance, and both wore their hair long.

Her transfer to her adoptive family

In pre-independence Singapore, large families were the norm. Contraceptives were only distributed to married women who approached clinics for medical advice or treatment or who were inflicted with tuberculosis, heart disease, diabetes, and other health complications, because of which childbearing was likely to endanger their life as well as their baby's. Thangah's biological parents had eight children altogether. Her father had five more children of his own from a previous marriage, three of whom were taken away by his first wife. Left with two children, he eventually remarried and had eight more children from his second marriage. With too many children to feed, Thangah was given away at five months of age.

As a child, to the bewilderment of her biological parents, she was constantly ill. One day, at the suggestion of a relative, her mother consulted a fortune-teller at the wet market. After selecting a few tarot cards from the deck—a common divination tool used by Chinese fortune tellers—the news came: the child had to be given away before ill fate descended upon the family. The ideal situation would be to give the child to 'an outsider', preferably a non-relative or even a non-Chinese family, uttered the fortune teller. If Thangah's biological mother did not heed this advice, the fortune-teller warned her, Thangah would eventually 'eat up' her father. It was a euphemism for saying that she might eventually cause her father's death if she stayed with the family. While this was the advice of the fortune-teller, the reality of the situation presented a more compelling reason for transferring her out of the family. Thangah's biological parents had to live on one meagre income. Thangah's father was a car mechanic and feeding ten children was a huge struggle. So, acting on the suggestion of the fortune-teller, Thangah's mother took the difficult decision of giving her up.

Residing in the same *kampong* was a childless Indian couple whom Thangah's parents befriended. Aware that Mr Ramasamy and his wife, Veeramah, did not have any children of their own, her biological parents asked them if they would take Thangah.

To their delight, Mr Ramasamy and his wife responded positively to the idea of receiving Thangah. On the day Thangah was handed over to her adoptive parents, she was accompanied with gifts of an *angpow* (red packet or red envelope containing a monetary gift given as a blessing) of five Singapore dollars, flowers, and some Chinese cake. It was a significant sum in 1952, especially for a poor family. Five Singapore dollars could have gone a long way in buying food and other basic necessities for the family—a *kati* or 604 grams of rice would have cost fifteen cents at that time.

Discovering the truth about her adoption

In her formative years, Thangah had no inkling that she was adopted. No one around her—her teachers and classmates, who were mostly Indian and Malay—ever queried about her ancestry despite her looking very different from her adoptive parents. It was only at twelve years of age when she had to 'make her IC' (identity card) in school that she came to grasp the truth—her adoptive parents were not her 'real' parents. The day before the IC officer came to school, her form teacher instructed all the students in the class to bring their birth certificate for proof of identity. She remembers vividly taking her birth certificate and carefully keeping it in her school bag after receiving it from her adoptive father. She also recalls not bothering to even look at the document closely as she assumed that her adoptive parents were her 'real parents'.

The shock came the day after. When the officer asked if she was Chinese, she was surprised and quickly retorted that she was Indian, refusing to believe that she was not of Indian origin. He then told her that that would be impossible since her parents' names, as indicated on her birth certificate, were obviously Chinese. They were Mr Koh Kwong Chong and Ms Yeo Siang Choo, respectively, while she had been born with the name of Koh Siew Kiang. These details were never changed since her adoptive father could not afford to hire a lawyer to process a new birth certificate to include his as well as his wife's names. Hearing that, Thangah quickly grabbed the document from his hand. Staring at it, she came to the realization that the officer was not lying. She was indeed of Chinese origin! Because she could not produce the details of her biological parents as well as siblings, she was not given a red IC befitting Singaporean citizens but a blue IC instead.

Having made this discovery, Thangah, being quiet and obedient by nature, decided not to broach the matter of her origin with her parents even though the incident had left her confused. She went on to say that since 'Indian girls are taught to be reserved and not ask questions', she thought it best not to pursue the matter. Although choosing to bottle up her feelings, nonetheless she was tempted to ask them if indeed she was Chinese. Later she decided to drop the idea.

As the years passed, holding a blue IC posed several problems for Thangah, especially since it did not contain details such as where she was born. Despite feeling restless about how everyone around her held a red IC, she felt helpless. But it was only after several years had passed that she began to recollect how a neighbour had said in passing that she knew her biological parents and brother. She was around twenty years of age at that time. She had always wondered what that meant. One day after school, she rushed home to query her neighbour about the whereabouts of her biological relatives without the knowledge of her parents. Her neighbour asked for a day or two to secure the details. The day after, Thangah met up with her again. On a piece of paper were the names of not only her biological parents but also her biological siblings and their address.

Armed with that piece of paper, Thangah rushed home and spoke to her parents of her desire to contact her biological relatives. She told them that she needed to ascertain her birthdate. It was incorrectly recorded in the document her father was given when he took the oath to become her guardian. The details in it did not tally with the information contained in her birth certificate—something which she thought should be put right so that she could apply for a red IC to become a Singaporean citizen. Besides that, she wanted to clarify the missing information regarding her nationality and country of birth in her birth certificate. It was not a stretch to say that her adoptive father was furious on learning about her intentions to contact her biological family. But that did not deter Thangah from going ahead to locate her biological family.

That Sunday, Thangah, accompanied by her adoptive mother and armed with the piece of paper on which was scribbled the address of her biological parents, went in search of her biological family. It turned out that they lived in an HDB estate in the MacPherson area not far from where she lived with her adoptive parents. The day she visited them would always be imprinted in her memory. Knocking on the door, Thangah could feel her heart pounding—not from fear or anxiety but a strange sense of excitement that she would be meeting her biological parents for the first time. Then, the door swung open, and there in front of her stood her biological mother. As Thangah and her adoptive mother were dressed in ethnic Indian clothing—her adoptive mother in a *saree* and she in a *pavadai* or half *saree*—her biological mother assumed that they were looking for an Indian family. The first response of her biological mother was, 'Oh, you come to the wrong house. The Indian family you are looking for live on the fifth floor.' Knowing that she was at the right home, Thangah went on to explain who she was and then quickly showed her biological mother the list of names jotted down on the piece of paper she was holding in her hand. At that point, Thangah's biological mother realized who she was.

Although taken by surprise, she immediately invited Thangah and her adoptive mother into the flat. Thangah's biological father and her brother, who were at home at that time, burst into tears of joy when they saw her. It was also during that encounter that Thangah learned why she had been given away. There was no anger on her part although she had suffered the ill fate of being separated from her biological family at such a young age. Rather, as she was processing her emotions and trying to understand the circumstances under which she was given away, she was struck by the joy of their having met her after all these years. She could sense that her biological father, in particular, was guilt-stricken for having given her away.

That afternoon Thangah made the startling discovery that Fatimah was her own biological sister. She was given to Mr Ramasamy and his wife in 1953, the year after Thangah was transferred. But fearing that they could not raise two children, after a few months had passed, Thangah's adoptive parents transferred Fatimah to a Malay couple who lived in the same *kampong*. Not only were they neighbours, but they were also tuck shop vendors at the same school: Geylang Malay Girls' School, where Mr Ramasamy sold *kacang puteh*—an assortment of fried nuts served in paper cones usually eaten as a snack, while the Malay couple sold Malay fare. As with Mr Ramasamy and his wife, the Malay couple who received Fatimah were childless and so were thrilled at the idea of receiving Fatimah into their lives. That said, the conversation led to an inquiry on the part of her biological parents into Fatimah's whereabouts.

That same afternoon, Thangah was to also learn that her biological relatives had attempted to look for her by paying for a small advertisement to be featured in the Chinese newspapers. But alas, her adoptive parents were Indian and did not purchase or read the Chinese newspapers, and so were in the dark about Thangah's biological relatives' attempts to locate her. Thangah's biological mother also said that giving away Thangah and Fatimah was not an easy decision. Every day she would see Thangah and Fatimah playing together, and it would pain her to see them since she knew they were her own birth children.

Just like Thangah's biological parents, it was common for poor families to give away their girl children more than their boy children. This was in keeping with the cultural practice that having too many daughters did not bode well for the Chinese, who had a cultural preference for sons. Although these beliefs or customs might be thought to be strange or antiquated by others or even to those of the current generation, they made sense within the Chinese community in those times. Holding on to cultural beliefs was commonplace, especially amongst the early settlers in Singapore, perhaps as a means to help them cope with the stresses that came with migrating to a new land.

Moving out of Lorong Sungkai

That afternoon revealed more details of her biological family to Thangah. Soon after giving Thangah and Fatimah up to their adoptive parents, Thangah's biological family moved out of Lorong Sungkai to live in the newly constructed flats in MacPherson. Thangah would find out that one of the reasons for her biological family moving out of the area was because it pained Thangah's biological mother to see Thangah every day as she passed Mr Ramasamy's house. Moreover, she knew that Thangah was toiling away to help her adoptive father keep his *kacang puteh* business going, and she felt immensely sorry that Thangah was forced to lead a difficult life. As redevelopment swept through the area, both Thangah's and Fatimah's adoptive families also moved out of the *kampong*. In 1965, Fatimah's family moved to Geylang, but she kept in touch with Thangah, who would visit Fatimah every year for Hari Raya.

Meeting Fatimah and her mother

At the request of Thangah's biological father, Fatimah's mother and Fatimah accepted his invitation to meet with the family the following week. Like Thangah's adoptive parents, Fatimah's adoptive parents also never revealed to her that she was an 'adopted' child. Born Koh Siew Lang, unlike Thangah, who saw her adoption as a non-issue, Fatimah took it badly on learning she was adopted, making this discovery only as an adult. As with Thangah, a fortune-teller was consulted because Fatimah too was constantly ill as a baby. But there was another problem. She was considered inauspicious because her big toe was very small in comparison to her other toes. She was upset to learn that she had been given away, primarily because this fact was hidden from her by her adoptive parents. Instead she would have preferred her adoptive parents to have told her the truth. But as the years passed, she became more accepting of her adoption.

After Fatimah and her adoptive family met her biological parents, there were many occasions on which all three families would congregate. At one gathering, Thangah's biological mother made a surprise announcement that she was thankful that her daughters had been taken care of very well by their adoptive parents, and she would never take her children back from them. So, they should trust her and not worry unduly about the fate of their children. In the same breath, she assured them that if anything dire were to happen to Thangah, Fatimah, or their adoptive parents, Thangah and Fatimah would always be welcome to come back to the family. But Thangah did not think much of this statement because her roots were strongly tied to her adoptive family. She considered herself an 'Indian' and could not envisage herself being back with her biological family and living as a 'Chinese' woman. Following Indian customs was second nature to her. She spoke fluent Tamil, had fully embraced Hindu religious rites, and served only Indian food at home. Her closest friends at the Community Club with whom she volunteers regularly are mostly Indian.

Her adoptive father

Unlike her adoptive mother Veeramah, Mr Ramasamy was not pleased about Thangah meeting her biological relatives. In fact, he was livid that she had gone in search of them in the first place, probably feeling insecure that he might 'lose' her once she had discovered her 'real' family or that her biological family might successfully convince her to return to them. Although Thangah had met her biological relatives, she realized that it was only with her adoptive parents that she had a deep and enduring bond. She had been an only child to her adoptive parents until she was twenty, which was when she had discovered her biological relatives. But Thangah implicitly knew the extent of the love her adoptive parents had for her. Her bond with her adoptive parents was strengthened further by the fact that her adoptive mother had lost a baby boy after a fall one day, after which her adoptive mother never became pregnant again. At that time, the only thought Thangah had was of having a younger sibling to play with since she was the only child. But that dream was shattered.

There was another context that nurtured the deep bond she had with her adoptive family. She recalls lucidly how she would help her adoptive father sell *kacang puteh* at the Kallang Wonderland on Sundays. Her mother would pack lunch for both of them in a little tiffin carrier. Thangah recalled how her father would eat first, after which he would have her eat his leftovers from the same food box. In accordance with Indian custom, usually the wife eats her husband's leftovers, and, in this case, the sharing of saliva was acceptable. But in Thangah's and her adoptive father's case, it was a daughter who was consuming her father's leftovers, possibly in an attempt to create a link between them since they were not biologically related. But Thangah never ever questioned her adoptive father's wishes nor his love for her. While Thangah had a deep love for her adoptive father, she found him strict.

She was always afraid of doing something that would rile him. It was often the case with girl children, with parents fiercely guarding their daughters, while their sons were given much more freedom and autonomy. Hence, Thangah would never do anything that would upset him.

Visiting her biological father

In the aftermath of discovering her biological family, on Sundays when she was not working with her adoptive father, Thangah would be found visiting her biological parents at the insistence of her biological father. During those visits, Thangah's father would always give her an *angpow* of fifty Singapore dollars and gifts of food such as chicken essence and the like. He did the same for Fatimah. When the factory she was working in was shut down for a few months, he made it a point to give her fifty Singapore dollars, apart from gifts of fruits, every time she visited him. Realizing that the money actually came from her biological siblings, Fatimah refused to take it once she returned to work. But Thangah and Fatimah were cognizant of one thing—that their biological father's actions towards them was hugely emotional. They were aware that he deeply regretted giving them away and was doing everything within his powers to forge the parental relationship he never had with them when they were growing up.

One day, during one of Thangah's and Fatimah's visits, Mr Koh suggested that a family portrait be taken. Thangah and Fatimah were agreeable to the idea and so were all their biological relatives, but not Thangah's father. He dismissed the invitation and decided not to go. For the photoshoot, Thangah's biological father insisted she wear a dress—he had been bringing her to the tailor to have her measured and was getting new dresses sewn for her regularly. Although Fatimah did not mind joining in the photoshoot, she was reluctant to wear a dress, saying that since she was Malay and Muslim, she would only wear a *baju kurung*.

Her marriage

Thangah's relationship with her adoptive father would be strained for a second time, this time concerning the man she wanted to marry. Thangah had met him through a girlfriend. They were both working in Texas Instruments, a semiconductor company established in Singapore in 1969, known also for manufacturing electronic parts and components. Thangah had landed a job in the company as a result of her eldest biological brother, William, providing her with an introduction. He was concerned for her and wanted to see her financially independent. Although Thangah was pleased to have landed a 'proper paid job', this infuriated Mr Ramasamy, who felt that Thangah had abandoned him. But her life would go on, and Thangah was delighted that the job gave her the opportunity to meet new people and make new friends, eventually opening the door for her to meet her husband-to-be.

It was a 'love marriage', something quite out of the ordinary in the Indian community since most marriages were arranged by parents. Jayakrishnan had spotted her at the Mariamman Temple along South Bridge Road during a three-month long festival culminating in the *Theemithi* or firewalking ceremony. It was a Hindu practice in which devotees walked across the firepit to be granted a wish or blessing by the Goddess Draupadi. Jayakrishnan was a devotee of the goddess, and she had volunteered to serve food to the devotees participating in the firewalking ceremony. It was literally love at first sight for him, as he muttered to himself, 'OK, I want to marry this girl one day.'

Since his brother knew Thangah's girlfriend's mother—the girlfriend with whom she had developed a strong friendship at Texas Instruments—it paved the way for them to be introduced to each other. In fact, Thangah says that if not for that introduction, she might not have been married because she was a rather reserved and shy person who did not socialize much, except for the few friendships she had developed in her job at Texas Instruments.

It was only later in the 1990s, when she started to volunteer at the Community Club, that she began to open up and talk more freely to people. She went on to say that that was how Tamil girls were brought up. Parents were very protective of their daughters, and girls were expected to be modest. Young girls of marriageable age would never attend weddings since it might incite others in attendance to ask if she was available for marriage. If a couple was invited to a wedding, a man would only bring his wife. Given the conservative upbringing Thangah had, going out with a man whom her adoptive parents did not approve of would have been the last thing she might have done.

But someone had infuriated Thangah's father by telling him that Thangah was lying and that instead of doing overtime on Sundays to earn extra income, she was actually out seeing a man. The most embarrassing incident was when her father publicly accused her of having a relationship behind his back. Not being able to take the shame, the next day Thangah vowed to end her life. Taking a glass of bleach in her hands, she thought it might be the best way of solving her problem. But instead of killing herself, she ended up in hospital with a tube in her mouth to drain out the bleach. After that experience, she was certain that she would never do anything again to cause self-harm.

Instead, she decided to move on in life. In a brazen move and without seeking the blessings of her adoptive father, she went ahead and married the man of her choice. Her marriage, held at a Hindu temple, was not attended by her adoptive parents. That was expected since her adoptive father disapproved of her decision to get married while her adoptive mother was in India at the time. Instead, the marriage ceremony was attended only by her biological relatives.

It was 30 March 1975, and Thangah was twenty-three years old. After consulting an astrologer, the wedding was held at 7.30 a.m. as it was deemed to be an auspicious time for the ceremonies to take place. At the temple, vegetarian food was served after the wedding ceremony. The food was simple, consisting of *idli*, *dosa*, some chutneys, and vegetable curries—essentially what was called tiffin food. Thangah recalls that apart from the expenses incurred for the ceremony, food served to the wedding guests, her silk saree, and the gold jewellery she wore, she had spent around 2,000 SGD.

That evening, there was a dinner celebration at the Islamic Restaurant, sponsored by her husband's magnanimous boss in the shipping company he worked for, called Fernando & Sons. In those days, dining at the Islamic Restaurant along North Bridge Road opposite the Sultan Mosque was a marker of status as only the middle class could afford to dine in such restaurants, let alone host a wedding dinner party. As Thangah recalls, back then, wedding receptions were either held at the temple or at home. It is not like today where it is the norm for wedding receptions to be held at banquet halls or ballrooms in hotels. For fifty guests— which included her husband's relatives and her own extended kin—the bill came to a little more than 1,000 SGD.

Although she was able to get the approval of her biological relatives for the marriage, it saddened her that her adoptive father was against the idea of her marrying the man she loved. And what was the reason? It turns out that Thangah's fiancé was from the Padayachi sub-caste or *jati*, as it was called. For Thangah's adoptive father, who hailed from Tamil Nadu in India, the fact that she chose a man from a lower caste brought great shame and a loss of face to him. He himself was from the Kallar caste, a higher caste amongst the Tamils. That said, it is possible that although Thangah was an adopted child, he never saw her as a 'Chinese' but rather as an 'Indian' girl—a daughter who was part of the family and who shared his caste. He could have also seen marriage as a way of incorporating his adoptive daughter into the Kallar caste, if she had married a man within the same caste. Amusingly, in this case, it would have been a Teochew girl becoming an 'Indian' girl of the Kallar caste!

Reconciliation

Starting her married life without the approval of her adoptive father was tough for Thangah in the beginning because of the strained relationship between herself and her adoptive father. They had not spoken to each other for exactly one year. But after the birth of her first child in March 1976, her adoptive father had a change of heart. He was elated that a son was born! One day, he asked to see the child, and dutifully Thangah and her husband visited her adoptive parents with their newborn infant. Her adoptive father was overjoyed upon seeing his grandson, and the child was gifted a gold chain and locket. The fact that she had a son was revealing. For Indians, having a son is significant. Boys are important to carry the family name, as it is with the Chinese. But having a son is important for another reason: at the funeral ceremony of a Hindu, the eldest son played a crucial role. Soon after the birth of her first son, a daughter and then another son were born.

Her 'Chinese' family

Throughout her married life, she continued to stay in touch with her biological family. They have been very much an important part of her family life in spite of the cultural differences between herself and them. Every year for Chinese New Year, the entire family, as well as her extended kin, gather at her biological family's home for the reunion dinner on the eve of the New Year, as it is customary amongst the Chinese for immediate family members to gather to celebrate the start of the Lunar New Year. In the Koh household, a hotpot or steamboat is always served as the main dish. Since they have a potluck celebration every year, each female member of the family was expected to bring a dish or two to share. While Thangah, her husband, and their children do not have food restrictions except for refraining from the consumption of beef, Fatimah always brought her own food.

She could not partake of the dishes shared by her biological relatives since they would have not been *halal.* Even after the passing of their biological father, nothing has changed: the entire family, including their children and grandchildren, continue to gather over Chinese New Year.

While Thangah joins her Chinese relatives as an expression of her acknowledgement of her Chinese roots, in her day-to-day existence, Thangah feels every bit an Indian woman. Fatimah's response has been the same although, for her, her Malay identity has superseded her Chinese background. So, it is not surprising that Thangah's biological relatives refer to her affectionately as the 'Indian sister' while Fatimah has come to be known to them as the 'Malay sister'. But to Thangah, Fatimah has always been her favourite sister and will always be so since they were playmates growing up. The feeling is mutual. For Fatimah, Thangah would always hold a special place in her heart and her life—a bond that would never change in spite of discovering the truth about their adoption.

Thangah was married in a Hindu ceremony held at the Sri Krishnan Temple in 1975, with her biological parents playing a key role in the ceremony.

A studio portrait taken in 1972 with Thangah's multicultural family. To the far right seated in the front row is Fatimah while Thangah, clad in a saree, is standing in the back row. Her adoptive mother, too, is in the picture, seated in the front row.

Chapter 8

The Woman I Am

Following the war

The years during which the Japanese occupied Singapore were difficult for most people. Poverty rates were high, and there was a great deal of suffering. Acute shortages of food were the norm, and basic consumer goods were difficult to come by. Amidst the human suffering, families continued to be large, and many people could not provide for their children adequately. This, in turn, led to a lot of children being put up for adoption by their biological parents. When couples wanted to give away their children fearing that they could not provide for them, seldom were these children given to 'total strangers'. Even if they were, the children were often given to a family with some degree of affluence, a family that could provide a loving and caring home.

It was after the Japanese occupation that Saraswathi Nagalingam was given away while she was an infant. In 1949, she was adopted by an Indian family. Her adoptive parents hailed from Tamil Nadu in south India and migrated to Singapore with their only daughter, who was a little girl at that time. One could say that they were a well-to-do family. Mr Nagalingam was a businessman who ran an import–export enterprise between Singapore and India. Her adoptive mother, Mrs Nagammal, was a full-time homemaker for the most part. However, she would buy sarees from Sithi Vinayagar saree shop in Serangoon Road and sell them to the wives of workers employed at Keppel Harbour, who lived around Everton Park and Kampong Bahru Road. This way, she would make a small profit to supplement the family income. They were typical early immigrants who came from India. They travelled back and forth rather than making Singapore their permanent home. Because of the business her adoptive father ran, the family ended up renting a shophouse space along Race Course Road.

Schooldays and her upbringing

Growing up, Saraswathi was a happy and contented child— obedient and disciplined. As she describes it, her upbringing was, for the most part, sheltered. She never went out on her own, aside from going to school. Her adoptive mother was a central figure in her life and strict in many ways—whenever she went out, she would always wear a *pottu* or 'a coloured dot worn on the forehead'. This was a habit Saraswathi was to adopt as she grew up. Her parents were as overprotective of her as much as they were of her adoptive sister Meenachi, who was eighteen years older than her. In fact, her adoptive sister was married off in 1944 at the age of thirteen to a man who was twenty-five years older. The uncertainty of the war was probably the reason that pushed her adoptive parents to consider marrying Meenachi off at such a young age, seeing it as a way to protect her. At that time, whether any person would survive was anyone's guess. She had also hit puberty, and, in Tamil culture, girls were married off as soon as they reached that age.

For Saraswathi, however, her life journey was to turn out very differently. At first she attended Owen School. Then, after doing really well in her first year, she was transferred to Raffles Girls' Primary School. After that, she studied at Fairfield Methodist Girls' School. Saraswathi was diligent in her studies and enjoyed science and mathematics, in particular. She still remembers her Mathematics teacher, Ms Krishnan who was a gifted teacher and had a flair for getting students to enjoy learning the subject in spite of the fact that it was not the easiest of subjects to excel in. Geography was another of her favourite subjects as it piqued her curiosity about the world that we live in. As for Tamil, it was a fairly easy subject for her since she spoke the language at home. Her teacher was Mrs Raman, who, Saraswathi thinks, was responsible for her love of the language. Her adoptive mother would guide her through her Tamil textbooks, but Saraswathi knew that because she was not highly educated herself, there was a limit to how much help she could provide. But that said, Saraswathi would always pass the subject with flying colours, making her mother proud.

Realization about her adoption

The moment of reckoning came when she was twelve. It was time to get her identity card (IC) processed. Her form teacher instructed the entire class to bring their birth certificates to school with them the next day. On arriving home, Saraswathi quickly informed her adoptive mother that she needed her birth certificate and why she needed it. Instead of handing Saraswathi's birth certificate to her, her adoptive mother insisted on handing it directly to Saraswathi's form teacher the following day. Saraswathi, however, thought nothing of her adoptive mother's course of action or why she thought it would be better if she handed over the document personally.

The following day, being busy with household tasks, it slipped her adoptive mother's mind that she had to collect Saraswathi's birth certificate from her form teacher. When her mother forgot to show up, her form teacher passed the document back to Saraswathi instead. Her form teacher probably thought that since Saraswathi was already twelve, she would be responsible enough to bring the document home safely.

That was the first time Saraswathi had the document in her hands. On looking at the document closely that she was overcome with shock. Why did it not have 'Saraswathi d/o T. Nagalingam' written on it? Instead, the birth certificate belonged to a woman by the name of Mary Teo. She also noticed that her adoptive father's name did not appear on the document. Instead, there was the name of a Chinese man under the column stated 'Father'.

Her first instinct was to question if the correct birth certificate had been returned to her. Although thinking that there might have been a mistake, she decided that she would take the document home and hand it over to her adoptive mother. Not knowing what to make of this 'discovery', the first thing she did was to ask her mother about the discrepancy in the names and if she was indeed of Chinese origin. Her adoptive mother, however, dismissed her questions and insisted that there was a mix up, advising her not to dwell on the incident.

But her battle with who she really was only grew after that episode. In school, whenever her name was called out by the form teacher while taking attendance, she could hear some of her classmates whispering to her: 'You are Chinese; you are not Indian,' as if her classmates were taunting her. Detesting these comments, she would go home and tell her adoptive mother about how her classmates verbally assaulted her, displaying her irritation. Crying to her adoptive mother, she would plead and say, 'Paint me black—I don't want this skin colour.' Saraswathi remarks that 'she often forgets how she looks like until someone tells her she is Chinese'. She has always wanted to be an Indian, and, for her, there was no reason for her to think otherwise.

More about her adoption

Saraswathi continued to have an unsettling feeling about her origin. She knew 'at the back of her mind' that she might be Chinese, as stated in her birth certificate. She was conscious of the fact that she looked different from her adoptive family. This always played on her mind. Aside from the information revealed to her in her birth certificate, her suspicion was only going to be fuelled further by a comment she received from a tuck shop vendor, 'I want to tell you—you are not Indian, you are Chinese!'

Plucking up courage, one day she decided to pose the same question she had asked her adoptive mother to her adoptive father. To Saraswathi, he seemed more receptive than her adoptive mother, whom she saw as a dominant personality in the home. It was then that he replied, 'You might not be our own child, but you are every bit our daughter, and I want you to take care of us when we grow old.' That settled her concerns. In fact, not once did her adoptive mother ever mention that she had no biological ties with Saraswathi. Perhaps that was why she wanted to keep the adoption a secret. Saraswathi had a deep sense of realization that her adoptive mother only wanted her to be her own. Since then, Saraswathi did not raise the story about her adoption again with them and neither did she tell anyone about her conversation with her father that day. Although she does not know the reasons why she was given away, she made up her mind that very same day that she would never broach the matter of her adoption with her adoptive parents again and would treat them as her own parents and nothing less. As her adoptive parents grew old, she kept her promise and took it upon herself to provide care for them.

University, marriage, and work

After completing secondary school, Saraswathi's father had plans of sending her off to south India to complete her studies. She first completed her pre-university, followed by obtaining a Bachelor of Science degree. As well as wanting her to receive an education, little did she know that her adoptive father had an ulterior motive for sending her to India. His plan was to get her married off to a man of the *Mudaliar* caste, the caste to which her adoptive parents belonged. On making this discovery, Saraswathi did not react violently, nor was she overtly upset with him, especially since she knew that amongst Indians, marriages were arranged. Instead, she knew deep down how much he loved her and only wanted the best for her. But given the fact that she was in India, and she saw how tough life could be and how different it was from Singapore, she could only breathe a sigh of relief that she never settled down in India. And, much to her delight, the man whom her adoptive father wanted her to marry had already been married off to someone else. And so, her life continued.

After completion of her studies, she returned to Singapore with her mother while her father stayed on in India. In Singapore she found a job at the F.E. Zuellig, a Swiss multinational company, and started working in the office as an assistant accounts clerk. It was there that she met her husband-to-be, Mr Somasundram, who was an accountant working in the same department. But that was not the first time she had met him. He had taken two classes at a remedial school she was attending when she was in secondary school. With a smile on her face, she says that perhaps they were 'fated for each other' and that's why life would bring them together again after so many years. Unlike many Hindu couples who would have consulted a Hindu astrologer to ascertain their compatibility as a couple before getting married, that idea never crossed the minds of Saraswathi and her husband-to-be. But as life would have it, her adoptive mother passed on before her wedding. Her father, fortunately, was still with her and was able to see her settle down with a man whom she chose to love. Saraswathi married Mr Somasundram in 1976 and later had two boys: the older became a pilot in 2007 with Singapore Airlines; the younger has been a mathematics and science tutor since 2002.

Looking back, Saraswathi says that she could never have married a Chinese man. Having been raised as an Indian, she feels like an Indian and identifies herself as one. She is acutely aware that her adoptive mother would not have been able to accept her denying her Indianness. An incident from the past always stuck in her mind. It occurred when she was in secondary school. Her mother became insistent on her wearing a *pottu* on her forehead so as to set her apart from her Chinese classmates. It was at that time that a series of race riots erupted in Singapore between the Chinese and the Malays. It was in 1964. Fearing that her daughter would be mistaken for a Chinese and her life might be endangered, Saraswathi's adoptive mother ensured that each time she left the house, she would wear the *pottu* on her forehead—that included going to school—to distinguish her as an Indian girl. At school, however, she felt increasingly uncomfortable wearing it since she was in a Christian environment. On entering the school compound one day, she cleaned the *pottu* off. To her dismay, she chose a day on which her adoptive mother would later pick her up from school. On meeting Saraswathi at the end of the day, her adoptive mother was horrified to find her without the *pottu*. On their journey back home, it was obvious her mother was extremely upset with her. Not a word was uttered between them. On arriving home, her adoptive mother complained to her adoptive father about what Saraswathi had done. Was she ashamed of being an Indian girl? Or was she ashamed of demonstrating her Indian heritage?

This incident lived on in Saraswathi's memory for a very long time. Until today, she always wears a *pottu*—not because of the incident she had had with her adoptive mother but because she has grown to be proud of her Indian upbringing and identity.

Her godmother

It was only as she grew older that more information about her adoption came to light. Mrs Mary Pitchay, who was a neighbour of the family—she had her home along Beach Road—as well as a confidante of her adoptive mother, was to play a key role in revealing details about Saraswathi's past. Although the whole idea of godparents was not in Hindu culture, Saraswathi would go on to hold Mrs Pitchay in high regard, calling her her godmother. It was she who acted as a mother to Saraswathi, providing her with moral and emotional support when first she lost her adoptive parents and later her husband, who left her a widow at the age of forty-six with two teenage boys to provide for.

Saraswathi recalls that she might have been a young girl when a Chinese woman regularly paid the family a visit at their home. They were living in their Race Course Road home at that time. But every time this Chinese woman stepped into the house, Saraswathi recalled she would be told by her adoptive mother to go into her room and study or to go out and play. She was never allowed to see the face of this woman. But one day she heard her adoptive mother telling the woman that she was not to visit the family anymore. She did not understand what had led her adoptive mother to utter those harsh words. Being young at that time, Saraswathi was not able to string the pieces of the puzzle together. She had no idea who the lady was until adulthood. It was Mrs Pitchay who unravelled pieces of that puzzle for her, revealing that the Chinese woman was actually her biological mother. Could it be possible that her adoptive mother decided to cut off ties with this woman as she did not want her to take Saraswathi back? The truth of the matter will never be known.

There was another incident that took Saraswathi through to a portal to her past. It was after school one day, and she was waiting for her adoptive mother at the entrance to the school compound. She was seven years old. While waiting for her adoptive mother, a tuck shop vendor whom she recognized approached her and started a conversation. She asked if Saraswathi was going home. Politely Saraswathi informed the woman that her 'mother' would be coming to pick her up soon, although evidently, she was late. Gently looking down at the child, the lady opened her purse and placed a 50-cent coin in Saraswathi's hand. She then told Saraswathi to take care of herself before parting ways. Later she was to learn from her godmother that the lady, who was Chinese, was none other than one of Saraswathi's older biological sisters who was running a stall in the school canteen. That encounter, however, was never to be repeated even though she continued to attend that school for another year.

As Saraswathi grew older, she was able to join the dots. It was crystal clear to her that her adoptive mother knew her biological family, according to what her godmother had related to her. At birth, Saraswathi was not given to total strangers. Instead, she realized, she was given away to a family whom her biological relatives were acquainted with. At that time, she surmised that her biological family had resided in a house along Upper Dickson Road since their address was indicated in her birth certificate. That she was born in a house in Little India was also a curious fact since her parents were living in Race Course Road, not far from Upper Dickson Road. In her birth certificate was another interesting detail. Although the document contained her father's name, it revealed that he was deceased at the time of the registration of her birth. This led Saraswathi to believe that she might have been given away because her father passed on, making her an inauspicious child according to Chinese cultural beliefs. Although she had sufficient information to go in search of her roots, there was never a time when she yearned to track down her biological family. Since then, she has not felt the need to seek out her past, being content with where she has arrived in life.

Her godmother, Mrs Pitchay, was a gentle and compassionate soul who wanted to share the details of Saraswathi's adoption with her only after the passing of her adoptive mother. She knew that if she had done so earlier while Saraswathi's adoptive mother was alive, that would only have hurt her adoptive mother deeply. Since then, Saraswathi 'has never been bothered to find out' where her biological relatives might be, nor did she go in search of them. In fact, a friend of hers—also a Chinese woman adopted into an Indian family—found her biological family after putting up an advertisement in the *Nanyang Siangpau*, a Chinese newspaper. She later encouraged Saraswathi to do likewise. But Saraswathi was unlike her friend in so many ways. She had no deep yearning to locate her biological family. There was a time, however, when her own husband remarked whether the family should go in search of her biological relatives. Saraswathi fended off his idea, telling him that she had no such intention, and the matter should be dropped.

Saraswathi speaks of how wonderful her life has been, as much in childhood as in adulthood. It was because of her adoptive parents that she was given the opportunity to pursue a higher education and to succeed in making a good life. She reflects that if not for them, her life might have turned out very differently. But for now, she is only grateful to her adoptive parents for the love and kindness she received from them and is indebted to them for making her the woman she is today.

Saraswathi's adoptive mother with her biological daughter are to the right of her while her adoptive sister and her son are to her left.

This studio photo was taken when Saraswathi turned ten years old.

Saraswathi with her adoptive father and mother.
The photo was taken because her adoptive father had turned sixty years of age.

This was a studio shot taken of Saraswathi and
her husband, Somasundram, in 1976.

Chapter 9

The Blue Bag

Her adoptive parents

Toshiko Kadir was the fourth child in the family she was adopted into. Toshiko's adoptive father, Peter Toshio Uyeda, was of mixed heritage—one-half Indian Muslim and the other half Japanese. Hence he bore the surname Kadir, a Muslim name since his own father was Indian Muslim. His mother was from Nagasaki, Japan, and had migrated to Singapore, where she ran a bar. It was in Singapore that she met Toshiko's paternal grandfather, Achmad Abdul Kadir, whom she would fall in love with and eventually marry. Toshiko recalls that her adoptive father looked very Indian. He wore the quintessential moustache, as it was a trademark for many Indian men, and had a sleek hairstyle. The only difference, however, was that he was exceptionally fair-skinned as compared to most Indians, the obvious reason being that he was of mixed parentage himself.

This was in contrast to her adoptive mother, Noepah Bolilak. She was much darker in complexion as she could trace her roots back to southern Thailand, being of Siamese stock. Her family had been displaced sometime in the early 1920s and settled in Ipoh in northern Malaysia, later moving further south into Singapore. Because of that, she was fluent in both the Thai and Malay languages but also spoke a smattering of Cantonese, which she had picked up through watching Cantonese movies and having a Cantonese nanny for several years. In Singapore, she ran a Thai restaurant which was frequented by the late Prime Minister Lee Kuan Yew and his siblings, as well as the Police Commissioner at that time, and other high-ranking police officers. Her marriage to Peter was her second, and so she had two daughters and an adopted daughter from her first marriage. One daughter would eventually marry into a minor royal family of Thailand—the Buranasiri. Thus, on Noepah's passing in 2014, she was bestowed a royal Thai funeral in Bangkok.

Growing up in the family, Toshiko always thought she was fair-skinned because of her paternal grandmother who was Japanese. Little did she know she was an adopted child with Chinese roots.

In school

Born in 1964, Toshiko grew up in a happy household. In her own words, she described herself as being 'spoilt rotten', being the youngest child in the family of four girls. She was the youngest in the family while her sisters were much older. Having had a middle-class upbringing as her father worked for Cathay Pacific in the ticketing department, she was a lively child and embraced life to the fullest.

She was born in the Katong area in Singapore and later grew up in Serangoon Garden, attending Cooling Close Convent and, later on, St Joseph's Convent. Active in extra-curricular activities in school, she was in the St John Ambulance Brigade and had many friends in school and continued to keep in touch with them into her adulthood.

In school, however, she would make it known to all her classmates that she carried a Japanese first name because she was a quarter Japanese through her father's side of the family. At least, this is what she thought of her own heritage and her origin. In fact, she took pride in the fact that her paternal grandmother was Japanese and made this known to all her friends whenever they inquired about the origin of her name. She was to learn later in adulthood that it was her Japanese grandmother who wanted her to be given a Japanese name so as to keep the 'connection with the family's Japanese roots'.

But, at that time, she did not know at all that she did not have 'one drop of Japanese blood' and neither did she have Thai biological links. Her classmates too saw her as exotic—having Japanese and Thai roots at the same time—and she enjoyed the attention of being different from everyone else. This was in the 1970s and 1980s.

But for the most part, the idea of being adopted never crossed her mind except for the one instance very briefly. It was in 1976, and the time had arrived for her to process her identity card (IC). She was told by her teacher that, unlike her classmates, she could not have her identity card processed in school. Reporting to her adoptive father that she needed her birth certificate, she was surprised when he responded that the family had misplaced it. She vaguely remembers that her adoptive father sought the assistance of a government department, and, some weeks later, a birth certificate was presented to her. She noticed it was a duplicate and not until her father's death did she find her original birth certificate and the adoption papers legalizing her adoption, complete with the names of her adoptive parents and her official new name.

Armed with her birth certificate, she could now apply for her identity card. While all her classmates had identity cards starting with the numbers S1634, Toshiko was bewildered that hers started with a different number. But what was more puzzling was that she was identified as an Anglo-Indian, possibly because in her father's identity card, he was categorized as a British Indian, since he was born at a time during which Singapore was a British crown colony. Since her father had that down, Toshiko surmised that the racial category of Anglo-Indian would have been the closest to being British Indian, and that was how she acquired her 'race'.

Work and marriage

Leaving college in 1982, Toshiko went on to work—first in the Civil Aviation Authority of Singapore or CIAS as a ground staff and after that holding several jobs, before settling down for a job at Club Méditerranée. Right before securing this job, she had travelled the world and decided to learn French through Club Med. It was through a mutual Belgian friend that she met her husband-to-be, Roland. There was 'instant chemistry' between them as they got on like a house on fire. Roland was the son of a successful Dutch father who was the right-hand man of Jan Pimm, the CEO of Philips at that time. He lived in Singapore— was twenty-six years old—and was the head of a division of a Swiss company, when he met Toshiko in 1987.

Assuming she was half Thai, her wedding was conducted with pomp in Thai tradition with monks chanting in the living room of her parents' house. The Thai-style wedding spanned two days, although the preparations for food started a day earlier. It involved the entire neighbourhood—the laborious effort of neighbours to help 'beat' fish into paste by hand; no one dared to suggest using a food processor! Toshiko also remembered that the feast included a Thai fresh fish laksa (dish stewed in coconut milk) cooked over five charcoal braziers and served to more than 150 guests who attended the wedding ceremony held in a tiny house. Aside from the glamorous fare, Toshiko was delighted to have been married in a Thai ceremony as she was under the impression that she was half Thai.

Confronting the reality of her adoption

It was the birth of her second son, whom she enthusiastically named Akio, that proved to be a turning point in her life.

Her dad was furious at the choice of the name, saying, 'How can you name him Akio!' But that seemed like the logical thing to do for Toshiko. 'After all, aren't I a quarter Japanese?' She and her husband were confounded at the opposition they received from her adoptive father to their choice of name for their second son. But that did not stop them from naming their second boy Akio. For them, it was a splendid opportunity of continuing and maintaining the Japanese connection.

Then came the shocking revelation. Toshiko's adoptive Chinese sister, who was sworn to secrecy never to reveal Toshiko's adoption by her own mother, decided to reveal the truth. Toshiko was neither Japanese nor Thai. But feeling guilty that she would be betraying her own mother, she broached this subject to Toshiko's husband, Roland, instead, leaving it to him to explain to Toshiko that she was an adopted child of Chinese origin.

To learn this truth was the greatest shock she ever experienced. It was four days after giving birth to her second son on 15 June 1991 that Toshiko, twenty-seven years of age at that time, found out that she had been fed a lie all her life. Not only was the truth about her adoption hidden from her, but she was to learn that all three of her sisters knew that she was adopted, and all three hushed up that fact. The reason for their not being forthright was discovered later. They were told to keep her adoption a secret so that she would never feel 'different' in the family. This was her adoptive mother's wish—the architect behind hiding the secret of Toshiko's adoption. And her sisters were quick to acquiesce to her instructions because they knew their mother was a strict woman and not someone whose wishes were to be opposed.

The reason for her adoption was something Toshiko was to learn later on. The story goes that her adoptive mother loved girls. So, when the prospect of receiving a girl child into the family came along, she was happy to give the child a home. Also, at that time, her adoptive mother was too old to have a child of her own in her marriage with Peter Uyeda. Hence, she felt that adopting a child with him would be just as good as having a child of her own with him. And it was not as if Toshiko was the first child she had adopted. Many years before that, she had adopted another Chinese girl during her first marriage.

After this, details about her birth parents slowly emerged. It was through one of her adoptive sisters—Mary, who is now in her eighties and who herself is adopted—that she found out that her birth parents lived in the same neighbourhood as her adoptive family and had a string of children. When Toshiko came along—she was the sixth child—they decided to give her up as they felt they could not keep her. Toshiko's adoptive mother, although illiterate, was loved and respected by everyone in the neighbourhood. She was the matriarch in the neighbourhood. If it was Vesak Day, she took it upon herself to organize the celebration of the festival, and no one would oppose her.

Toshiko's adoptive mother was 'very traditional' in many ways. She observed every Thai custom and festival throughout the year. In spite of living in Singapore, she never lost her Thai roots, and Toshiko gleefully celebrated every one of them, thinking she was part Thai. Toshiko's adoptive mother was the opposite of Toshiko's adoptive father in so many ways. He was a self-centred and penny-pinching but carefree individual. It was clear that it was her adoptive mother who made the final decision to welcome Toshiko into the family. It was no surprise that Toshiko's biological parents knew that giving her up to Toshiko's adoptive family was the right thing to do. They were confident that Toshiko would be well taken care of and provided for.

Another revelation

But those were not the only revelations Toshiko would learn about her adoption. The real shocker came a few years later. Soon after her adoptive father passed away, the house in

Serangoon Garden was put up for sale. Toshiko was summoned home to pack up her things for the move. Walking into her bedroom in the house, she was overwhelmed with emotion. Every one of her belongings was still where she had left it all those years back, first when she had moved out and then after she married Roland.

When she and her first son Antoine, who was twenty years of age then, were packing away her things, she chanced upon a blue bag. It contained several documents, including her original birth certificate. It was a large, greenish-blue document. While it did not look familiar to her, because it was a fairly large piece of paper, it caught her attention, and she decided to show it to her son. Scrutinizing it, Antoine thought it odd that the individual whose name appeared in the birth certificate shared the same birth date as Toshiko: 6 April 1964. But that was not all. The timing of the birth of that individual coincided with Toshiko's birth time: 1.43 a.m. How uncanny! It was the exact time of birth as Toshiko's. It was at that point that he realized that the person whose name appeared in the birth certificate was actually his mother. He then quickly announced his discovery. 'Mum, hello, it's you! Are you okay?'

It was at that very moment, with all those forces converging, that Toshiko suddenly realized that indeed she was adopted, confirming what her husband and her one sister had said to her a few years before that. And that the individual whose name appeared in the birth certificate was, in fact, herself—Lim Boh Phong. Toshiko thought that the name bestowed on her by her biological parents was positively ghastly, a name she could never have lived with. At that, Antoine quipped, 'Oh mom, aren't you glad you were adopted?' making the two of them burst into laughter. Looking more closely at the document again, Toshiko learned that her father was from China—Hainan Island, to be exact—while her mother was a Singaporean Chinese.

Refusing to live the lie

On looking back, Toshiko knew that she had been lied to. She also came to realize that while she was convinced that as a child she was the biological offspring of her adoptive parents, that was not the case. After all, she looked very different from them, different to the extent that it reinforced the fact of her being adopted. Although she herself was not aware of her adoption growing up, she was confident that everyone around her, including the neighbours, knew that she was adopted. But she was also sure that nobody would have dared to ask her adoptive mother regarding her adoption.

But Toshiko felt strongly that she would be lying if she continued to tell others that she was of Japanese or Thai descent. Since 15 June 1991—the day on which she came to realize the full extent of her adoption—Toshiko took an about turn concerning her roots. The time had come for her to tell her friends the truth about her heritage and identity. Since then, every time someone enquires if she is Japanese, she is quick to tell them, 'I'm actually not Japanese although I have a Japanese name.' She would take the opportunity to elaborate on the fact that she had been adopted into an Anglo-Indian, Japanese, and Thai family.

On discovering her roots

Because she was happy for most of her life, and her adoptive parents did not treat her any differently from her adoptive sisters but always treated her as their own, she does not 'feel anything' about being an adopted child.

Nothing in her life has really changed since discovering that she was an adopted child, and that her parents who raised her were not her 'real' parents. She has also come to accept the amount of orchestration on the part of her adoptive parents that kept the fact of her adoption a 'secret' from her. She does not make a big fuss about her adoption experience, especially since she is 'too old to even care about it'.

Currently, her curiosity as to who her real relatives are is only piqued when the issue of her adoption arises. At other times, she is curious, sometimes wondering if the woman standing next to her at the traffic lights might be her biological sister. She knows it might not be too difficult to track down her biological relatives. There were details in her birth certificate which made it possible for her to trace them. Toshiko's biological mother was thirty-six years old when she had Toshiko, so there is a good chance that she might still be alive today! And if not her mother, her siblings would certainly still be around. She is aware that she has several options if she wants to trace them. She can hire a private investigator, especially since she has the details of her birth, such as being born at the Khoo Maternity Clinic along Koon Seng Road; or she can feature her story in the newspapers or social media. In truth, she has never felt the need to go down that path in search of them and says that perhaps she is 'built differently' compared to other adopted children. They might find their biological family, only to be disappointed that they are nothing like the adopted child had expected them to be.

How she sees herself

Toshiko was shielded from knowing about her adoption until adulthood. While today, for the most part, Toshiko sees herself as ethnically Chinese, she is not able to fully understand what it means and feels to be 'Chinese' since her upbringing was mostly Thai and Japanese by culture while Malay and English were the languages spoken at home. Neither does she identify herself as an Anglo-Indian as she does not have European or Indian ancestry. For her, identity is complex, linked with upbringing more than how the government or others might come to define who an individual is. But if anyone is curious and asks her about her ancestry, she is quite happy to describe herself as a Singaporean Chinese adopted into a racially mixed family.

Toshiko's adoptive parents, a picture she cherishes
as it is framed and sits on her side table.

Toshiko at the age of six, a picture taken
on her graduation from kindergarten.

Chapter 10

Then There Were Two

The art of blending in

Walking down the main street of Little India—a vibrant, colourful quarter of Singapore dominated by the Indian community—it is not uncommon to see a glimpse of a Chinese woman attired in a saree or *salwar kameez*, draped in Indian jewellery, and wearing a *pottu*. If one were a visitor or stranger to Little India or Tekka, as the Tamils called the district, the initial reaction would be that of curiosity since her physical features in every way resemble those of a Chinese woman, and yet she looks completely comfortable in Indian attire and appears to know her way around the area well. What is also striking is that she would be speaking fluent Tamil as she mingles with the storekeepers and goes about her shopping weaving in and out of the side streets. At the same time, storekeepers around her seem unfazed by her 'looking different' from the rest of them as she haggles with them. They seem to consider her as part of the Indian community and not an outsider.

Mano's adoption

Although she looks every bit a Chinese, Mano Param always wears a *saree* or *salwar kameez*, strongly identifying herself as an Indian.

Born in Singapore in 1948, she was adopted by an Indian couple, Mr and Mrs Govindasamy, who had three sons of their own and sought to adopt a girl, hoping to have both male and female children. Her adoptive parents also thought that when they grew old, girls would make for 'better children' as they would look after them more than boys.

Mano's adoption occurred the year in which the eldest of her adoptive parent's sons drowned in a river along the 4.5 mile along Bukit Timah Road. His death was a tragedy for her adoptive parents since their son was only twenty-one years of age. He had just been engaged to be married when the accident occurred. This happened during the new year period when the rains would cause the canal to swell. His body was found further downstream near where the former University of Singapore was located. Mano's adoptive mother was shattered by the death. In the subsequent years, on the eve of the New Year, which was when her oldest son drowned, she would hold prayers at the very site where his body was found. On that day, a feast would also be offered for him to appease his soul.

It was only after adopting Mano that her adoptive mother came back to her old self, as if a light sparked within her. To her delight, she did not just welcome one child into her life but two: Mano and her younger biological sister. This was in 1952. Mano was four years old at that time, and her sister was a year younger than her. After adopting Mano and her sister, her adoptive mother would find herself with child after many years. Mano recalls how her adoptive sister was exceedingly pampered in her childhood. She realized that she was given preferential treatment in that she was never asked to do much housework, unlike Mano and her own biological sister.

In spite of how her adoptive mother felt towards her own biological child, Mano felt a strong sense of filial piety to her adoptive parents and what they had done for her and her biological sister. As a child, her adoptive mother would always remind her that there were other couples who also showed an interest in adopting her. But there was little doubt that she wanted both Mano and her younger sister, and these two girls brought immense happiness to her, especially after the loss of her son. In the depths of her heart, Mano knew that her adoptive mother would do anything for the two of them. That was the extent to which she was protective over Mano and her biological sister.

Her biological family

Later in life, Mano and her biological sister would learn that both of them were given away because their birth mother had passed on just after giving birth to twins. Of the twin siblings, the girl survived while the boy passed on. Unable to take care of all his children, her biological father had little choice but to give her away along with her younger sister. She was also aware that her eldest sister was given away to a Chinese family. There was a time when she, her younger sister, and oldest sister would get together very often and play over the weekends. However, she has no knowledge of the whereabouts of that sister today.

She also remembers her father visiting her and her biological sister when they were young. She might have been four years old then. Whenever he would visit them, he would hold the two of them tightly as he missed them dearly. Shortly after those times he visited Mano and her biological sister, she discovered that he would never visit again and was told by her adoptive mother that he had left for China for good. It was then that the reality of her adoption sank in. Although fairly reticent about her adoption, her adoptive mother would later tell her that her biological father lived along Dunearn Road. It was not far from where she had lived with her adoptive parents. Adam Place, at that time, was essentially a *kampong*. But sensing that her adoptive mother did not like to talk about 'things concerning her adoption' or her biological family, she dropped the idea of trying to glean more information from her, fearing that her questions would not be welcomed, and she would be seen as an unfilial child.

Her childhood

Although her adoptive parents were fairly strict with her and her biological sister, Mano described her childhood as a happy one. Her adoptive father worked as a gardener in the Botanical Gardens. On weekends, she remembers visiting the gardens with her biological sister and father. While playing in the gardens with her biological sister, at times she would see the late Prime Minister Lee Kuan Yew, exercising accompanied by his bodyguards. Although she was too young to recognize who he was, she would recall her father exclaiming in Tamil, 'Look . . . that's Mr Lee Kuan Yew. He's a very "big" man,' implying that he was a very important person in Singapore.

In her adulthood, the gardens would often bring back fond memories for Mano. She still recalls that while her father's colleagues would be meticulously trimming the plants and shrubs on the grounds—by then he had retired—she and her sister would run around and play with each other. As Mano and her sister wore pompom dresses or the *pavadai*—a blouse and long skirt often worn only by young girls—and had plaited hair, they attracted the attention of visitors who often ended up taking photographs of them.

In those days in the gardens, there used to be a canteen near the pond, which was later renamed Swan Lake. She still remembers how visitors could collect leftover bread from the canteen vendors to feed the fish. As Mano threw bread scraps into the pond, she would take delight in watching the fish surface to gobble up the bread.

For Mano, a visit to the gardens was a welcome outing for another reason. It was at the canteen that her adoptive father would buy her and her biological sister each a vanilla cupcake topped with lots of cream. As a young child, she still recalls how the cupcake was seen as a glorious treat from her adoptive father since food at home tended to be mainly Indian fare. She still recalls relishing every bit of the cupcake. She would first lick off the cream on top of the cake—starting with the leaves, followed by the flowers—and then devour the rest of the cake a little at a time.

Another memory of the gardens was the fact that it was a favourite haunt of visiting actors and actresses from India. Mano could rattle off the names of these movie stars even as a child. There was Shammi Kapoor, Padmini Ramachandran, and Ragini. She also remembered the movie *Singapore*, which was released in 1960, starring Shammi Kapoor and Padmini Ramachandran. During one of Mano's visits to the gardens, she was ecstatic to have met the actress Padmini in person, taking a stroll in the gardens after a movie shoot. During the encounter, she remembers Padmini asking her if she would like to visit India, to which she enthusiastically shouted with a resounding 'Yes'!

But the gardens were not the only place that brought back nostalgic memories for Mano. Going to the movies at the Diamond or the Royal cinemas was a popular outing for her adoptive family, just as it was for many amongst the Indian community. It was on Sundays that the morning shows at the Diamond Theatre were half price. After the show, Mano, her biological sister, and her adoptive father would have a meal at the Islamic Restaurant, a restaurant with a rich heritage dating back to 1921, established by the then Master Chef of the Alsagoff family and famous for its mutton and chicken *biryani*. They would then go to the Royal Theatre to watch another movie. Both the Diamond Theatre and the Royal Theatre, located along North Bridge Road, screened only Tamil movies. The Royal Theatre was much older than the Diamond Theatre and started off as a Malay theatre before starting to screen Tamil movies in the 1950s. Because of fires, both cinemas finally saw their closure in the 1970s.

Although an adoptive child, Mano had a special relationship with her adoptive mother. She still recalls affectionately how she would accompany her adoptive mother to visit the homes of her close relatives. In those days, she said, it was common practice to visit relatives at least once a month. But alas, this practice became less common as lifestyles changed and people prioritized careers over family life.

Schooldays

At first, Mano attended Duchess Primary School and then St Joseph's Convent for a term. Later she completed her secondary school education under the *Lembaga Gerakan Pelajaran Dewasa* programme at Monk's Hill Secondary School. She was an average student although conscientious in her studies. As she did well in Tamil, she was often praised by her Tamil teachers for scoring the highest marks amongst the cohort of students in primary school. She recounts the day on which her teacher took her aside and advised her to pursue a degree: 'Manoranjitham, you shouldn't stop at your O-levels . . . Singapore [University] doesn't offer Tamil but you can study Tamil at the University of Malaya . . . you should go there.' Instead of feeling a sense of achievement, Mano did not like the attention she received from her Tamil teachers since it caused some of her classmates to become jealous of her. It was also in school that Mano became conscious of her Chinese identity. She thought that if she were Indian, it might have been very different. But she was a Chinese and not an Indian; then how could she do better than the rest of the class who were Indian by birth? In fact, she still recalls how some of her Indian classmates responded to her success. They seemed to be annoyed, especially one particular lad. Although he would restrain himself in the classroom, the minute the bell rang and students exited the classroom, he would call out to her in a mocking tone in Tamil, saying, 'Chinathi, Chinathi, Chinathi,' which translates as 'Chinese girl' which he would utter in rounds of three. Ironically, as the years passed, they chanced upon each other in adulthood and became good friends.

The other instance in which her Chinese identity was highlighted was when her identity card was processed. Instead of including only her Indian name 'Manoranjitham d/o Govindasamy', she was given a choice to have her Chinese name included as well. This was possible until the 1970s when one could choose to add an alias in the card. And so, this document came to bear both her names: her Tamil name and her Chinese name— Tan Ah Moi. Ironically, under the column for ethnic group, her identity card states that she is Indian.

Marriage

On completing her O-levels, Mano chose to work instead of pursuing a university education. In 1971, her life changed. This was the year in which she got married. It was 9 July, and she was twenty-three years of age when she married S. Param at the Sri Krishnan Temple along Waterloo Street. From then on, she took on the name of Mano Param. It was a love marriage, unlike many Indian marriages that tended to be arranged. They had met at a jewellery store along High Street where she worked. This was the first street to be constructed in Singapore and was the shopping haven for the elite community residing in Singapore in the 1970s. At that time, her husband-to-be was working for B.P. De Silva, a luxury jewellery store based in Singapore and dating back to 1872.

Her adoptive father, however, was not very pleased at her choice—not because her husband was a Ceylonese Tamil but because there was an eighteen-year gap between them! Her father remarked that if she insisted on going ahead with the marriage, she 'must never come back home and cry to them' [meaning he and his wife]. While always holding that thought in her heart, she is grateful to God that she has had a good and fulfilling marriage. In spite of the age difference between herself and her husband, her marriage has lasted for more than fifty years. Mano went on to have a son, who eventually became the favourite grandchild of Mano's adoptive mother, while her husband, Param, continued to work in the jewellery business until retirement.

In those days, Indian weddings were a three-day affair. On the first day, the bride and groom's families would have separate religious ceremonies. Amongst the groom's family, the *thali*—a gold pendant which is a symbol of marriage—would be offered to the gods to be blessed. Separately, the bride's relatives would organize a *henna* ceremony, followed by a bangle ceremony, which only women relatives would attend. For the bangle ceremony, only certain female relatives would be allowed to help the bride put on bangles—sisters of the father or wives of the mother's brother(s), daughters-in-law of the couple's parents, and those considered sisters of the bride. The bride would have to wear the bangles—most of which were made of glass, interspersed with gold ones—until the wedding ceremony was over. The actual ceremony fell on the second day. Held either at the temple or at home, the groom tied the *thali* on the bride and the wedding was solemnized. On the evening of the second or the third day was the *oonjal*, when a dinner and reception ceremony would be organized for the couple. A decorated wooden swing would be set up for the bride and bridegroom to sit on while their relatives would rock them. Usually, two young girls would flank the swing and fan the couple. Relatives would also be involved in the various tasks related to the organization of the event, including the preparation of food, of which copious amounts would have been cooked to feed the many guests attending the wedding celebration.

Fancy dishes like *ghee* or clarified butter rice, chicken *korma*—a dish prepared with ground almonds, cashew nuts, and green chili and laced with spices, mutton *piratel*—a dry curry in which the meat is fried in chili, turmeric powder, and other spices, brinjal chutney, and cucumber *raita,* a chilled dish consisting of grated cucumber mixed with coconut milk were the usual fare, although the breakfast would have been vegetarian. A few days before that, a tent or *pantal,* made with natural materials such as coconut leaves to form a thatched roof and woven coconut leaves to form walls, would be constructed by the relatives. This was both functional as well as decorative. While this was a typical wedding for Tamil Hindus of the 1960s and 1970s living in Singapore, Mano did not have such an elaborate wedding because her adoptive father was not in favour of the marriage.

Her younger sister

Mano's younger sister, who was adopted by the same couple, was very different from her. In the past, her younger sister called herself Tan Ah Moy or went by her English name Rita rather than her Indian name Sithaletchmi. It was obvious that their adoptive mother found this to be insulting as her adopted daughter did not want to acknowledge her Indian identity. As she grew older, Sithaletchmi would only feel a greater emotional chasm between herself and her adoptive mother. For that reason, her adoptive mother would often ignore Mano's sister, commenting on several occasions that Mano was 'her loving daughter' who was faithful to her, unlike her sister, Sithaletchmi, who would choose instead to identify herself with the Chinese community in spite of being raised by Indians.

As she drifted away from her adoptive family, Sithaletchmi would regularly offer prayers to her biological mother as a 'guiding light' to her. When Mano visited Sithaletchmi in the

1980s in Cheras, Malaysia, where she and her husband had established a restaurant, her sister would often broach the idea of offering prayers to their biological mother, as an expression of their emotional bond with her. But her reminders would prove useless as there was hardly any chance that Mano would direct her affection from her adoptive mother to her biological mother. She was certain that she was not going to erect an arbitrary wall between herself and her adoptive mother.

Maintaining her Indian roots

Although Mano was often teased for being Chinese when she was young, she has always thought of herself as an Indian. Insisting on her Indian identity whenever anyone would inquire about her 'race', Mano has expressed her Indianness in a number of ways. As a child, visiting the temple was a regular affair since her adoptive parents were religious. In her adulthood, she would continue this religious practice. On public holidays, she would regularly volunteer at the Sri Senpaga Vinayager Temple along Ceylon Road and make guests feel welcome in the temple. Still she is a regular devotee at the temple and she has made many friends there.

Another way in which she projects her Indian identity is by excelling in the Tamil language. Her successful integration into an Indian family and, in turn, the Indian community takes the fullest form in her use of the Tamil language, the language of the ethnic group into which she was adopted. Seldom does she use the English language when meeting Tamil friends or fellow devotees at the temple. On all occasions, she prefers using the Tamil language as she feels comfortable using it.

Mano also steadfastly holds on to her Indian identity in her role as a grassroots leader in her constituency. Although coming in contact with grassroots volunteers from all ethnic backgrounds—

there are Chinese, Malay, and Indian volunteers—she never fails to identify as an Indian, if anyone broaches the topic of her identity. Moreover, for every activity run at the grassroots level, Mano turns up in a traditional Indian costume, such as a *saree* or *salwar kameez*, and top it off by marking her forehead with a *pottu*.

While she was not given away into a wealthy family, Mano recognizes her adoptive parents gave all they could to the best of their ability while raising both she and her biological sister. She is always grateful for the love and care they have showered on her. And her love for her adoptive parents is only amplified in her very being and existence and in how she has come to express her identity as an Indian woman.

Mano and her biological sister in 1957. Mano was nine years old while her biological sister, Sithaletchmi, was a year younger. This picture was taken after the ear-piercing ceremony held at home, attended by friends and relatives. To memorialize the event, a picture was taken at the studio later that day.

*Mano, her biological sister Sithaletchmi, her adoptive sister,
and a relative of her adoptive family.*

*Mano and her husband at her biological sister Sithaletchmi's
wedding. This photo was taken in June 1983.*

Mano, her husband, and their son (behind the couple) presenting offerings of coconut, fruits, flowers, and a garland for special prayers to the main deity at the Sri Senpaga Vinayagar Temple along Ceylon Road.

Chapter 11

Trustworthy Strangers

A tiger girl

It was 1938. In the sleepy town of Kulai in the Johor state of Malaya, a child was born to a young couple. Sadly, in the stillness of the night, the woman quietly took her last breath while her infant survived. With the passing of the woman, her biological family scrambled to decide if they should keep the child. It was the year of the tiger. Tiger girls had a horrendous reputation. They were considered strong, daring, and aggressive. In the case of Jane, she was to learn later in life that because her biological mother had died during childbirth, her family was forced to give her away. The belief was that she had 'eaten' her biological mother's soul and keeping her in her natal family would only bring further bad luck to them.

On hearing that a Chinese farmer was desperately needing to give away his newborn child, Daniel Joseph, a male nurse—or 'hospital assistant' as they were commonly known—and his wife, Grace, decided to take in the child. It was four days after Jane's arrival into this world that Grace made her way to the farmer's house to receive Jane. Arriving at their home, Grace received Jane in her arms from an elderly Chinese woman, presumably the mother-in-law of Jane's deceased biological mother. It was common for women to live with their husbands' families after marriage, in keeping with Chinese customs. While receiving Jane, Grace spotted a fairly young man with a scrawny body, standing in the corner of the living room, sobbing away. Could it have been Jane's biological father who was stricken with sadness because his daughter had to be given away?

As a young adult, Jane would later learn from her adoptive mother that an envelope containing fifty Singapore dollars was handed to her biological family, possibly for any expenses that might have been incurred before, during, and after her birth. The money was strictly a gift—an *angpow*, otherwise known as 'ginger and cake money'. In no way could a child be seen as being 'bought' and 'sold'. Fifty Singapore dollars at that time was considered a huge sum in terms of 'pre-war money' as 1 cent could buy someone a bowl of noodles. Jane's adoptive family could be considered people of means. Thus, they could 'afford' providing for another child since they had only one biological son, Anthony, who was nine years of age at that time. Although fifty Singapore dollars was hardly a paltry sum, it has been documented in some sources that some adoptive parents paid as much as 1,000 SGD for a baby! But if large sums were involved, as was the case when affluence had set in, particularly in the 1960s onwards, usually it was meant for the individuals who acted as brokers in facilitating the transfer of the child.

In the case of Jane's adoptive parents, there was no need for a broker. Jane's adoptive father was a well-known figure in the community, managing a dispensary in the Midland Estate run by the Japanese in the state of Johor while doubling as a homeopathy practitioner. Being a male nurse meant that people not only knew who he was, but they also turned to him for help, especially if they struggled with different bodily ailments. Because a broker was not involved in her adoption, it could be surmised that it was most likely members of the community who relayed the message to her adoptive father about the intention of her biological parent to give her up. And so began Jane's life journey in the home of her adoptive family.

Baptism and good fortune

While she cannot remember much about the formative years of her life, there was one thing that stuck in her mind: her parents provided a loving home for her and they were extremely protective of her. One of the first milestones of her life was her baptism. Although not remembering that incident as she was only three months old, Jane was aware that her adoptive parents, being practising Catholics, brought her all the way to Singapore to be baptized. Her baptism was held at the Our Lady of Lourdes Church on 25 July 1938 and the baptismal ceremony was presided over by Reverend Father Arokiasamy. At that time, Johor came under the Archdiocese of Malacca and Singapore, and since it was easier to get to Singapore from Kulai, it was more likely that her adoptive parents were advised to bring the child to be baptized in a church in Singapore. Till today, Jane has kept her baptismal certificate safely. For her, it was not just a religious document, but it affirmed who she was, her name, and her link to her adoptive parents. This document was to be of great importance to her in adulthood since she did not have a birth certificate. It was her baptismal certificate instead that indicated her full name and the names of her adoptive parents, who became formally acknowledged as her guardians.

Although Jane was baptized as Jane Felicia Joseph, a name which would later appear in all other formal documents, at home she was affectionately called Pakiam, which meant 'good fortune' in Tamil. It was a pet name used only amongst family members, extended kin, and close friends. It was later that she found out the reason she had been given that name. It seems that on the very day she arrived at the home of her adoptive parents, her father had won the lottery together with a handful of very good friends.

As she was believed to have had brought 'good luck' to the family on her arrival, subsequently, if anyone amongst her adoptive parents' friends bought a lottery ticket, they would come to their home looking for Jane. The lottery ticket would be placed in her hands in the hope that the number on the ticket they had purchased would be the winning number!

Surviving the Japanese occupation

Four years after she had been transferred as a child to Mr and Mrs Joseph, war broke out in Malaya. Until that time, Jane's adoptive family lived in the state of Johor. It was also then that her adoptive parents separated as they had irreconcilable differences. Her adoptive brother, separated from his biological parents, was sent to Kuala Lumpur to live with his paternal grandparents while Jane continued to live with her adoptive mother in Johor until the war ended.

As with her baptism, she has very little recollection of that time, although her adoptive mother told her about the anxiety she went through during the war. Every time Jane's adoptive mother heard the loud sound set off by the sirens reverberating across the sky, she described having to quickly scoop Jane off the ground and rush for the closest bomb shelter to hide. Her adoptive mother was more fearful for Jane's life than her own, she was later to learn. Jane was Chinese, a target of the Japanese unlike the Indians. Her adoptive mother was gripped with fear, having heard numerous lurid stories about how Japanese soldiers would kill Chinese children and babies by impaling them with their bayonets.

As the war ended and life returned to some sense of normalcy, an opportunity to be trained in midwifery at the Seremban General Hospital arose for Jane's adoptive mother. Seizing the opportunity to become a midwife, she started her training in 1946 at a British hospital, and by 1947, she had earned herself a certificate to practise midwifery after successfully completing her examinations, which were held in Kuala Lumpur that same year. Unfortunately, jobs were difficult to come by since, by then, the numbers of women in the villages wanting a home birth were declining. Many of them opted instead to seek gynaecological and obstetrical services at hospitals.

In Seremban Convent

After the war, Jane returned to school in 1947. In school, Jane remembers being stared at constantly. She did not quite understand why her classmates often looked at her with curiosity. She was also acutely aware that sometimes they would be whispering amongst themselves, although she came to suspect it might have been because of a mismatch between her name and her countenance. Although she had the appearance of a Chinese girl, her last name was obviously non-Chinese.

Putting that 'strange' experience aside, Jane enjoyed school for the most part. She attended the Convent of the Holy Infant Jesus in Seremban. However, she was older than most of her classmates since she had missed a year because of the war. One of the most vivid memories she has of starting school was her attempts at learning English as she mainly spoke Tamil at home. In Standard 1, she remembers having had lots of catching up to do. She recalls how a hospital colleague of her adoptive mother gave her private tutoring lessons to help her along. Initially, she found mastering the English language very difficult since Tamil was her native tongue. At that time, her form teacher in school was a Miss Goh Choo Kim. Jane liked her because she thought she was an exceptional teacher who was very encouraging and who inculcated in her the desire to pursue knowledge. This habit would stay with her into her adulthood as she self-taught herself to read Tamil by purchasing basic Tamil textbooks from Little India. Jane recalls her days in primary school with great joy.

Her favourite time of the school year was the start of the new year. She still remembers looking forward to her adoptive mother buying her the textbooks she needed for all her subjects. She enjoyed school immensely, in particular discovering new things about the world she lived in. One of her favourite pastime was reading all her books from cover to cover, even by candlelight, as there would be blackouts on some days.

There was also a family friend by the name of Mr Murugesu whom Jane remembers vividly. His little sister was a classmate of Jane's in the same convent school. Whenever he bought his sister exercise books and pencils, Jane too received the same gifts from him. He was a very kind man! Jane treasured those gifts. In Standard Two, she was still lagging behind in her studies. Yet Jane persevered. She remembers that period of her life vividly. Even at night, she would be reading her textbooks until she was fairly confident that she had a good grasp of their content. That year, her form teacher was Miss Annie Dragon. Jane thought she was a very sweet, gentle lady. Finally, in Standard 3, she could breathe a sigh of relief as her days of hard work had paid off. She finally 'topped the class'. To this day, Jane still remembers her form teacher, Miss Olga Prout, who was extremely pleased with Jane's progress and was very proud of her achievements.

At home, Jane occasionally wore the *pattu pavadai*—silk blouse with matching skirt—a native South Indian costume, during celebrations. Her adoptive mother would also braid her hair in plaits, which was common for Indian women and girls, and add a little *pottu* on her forehead. She earnestly thought she was an Indian like all her adoptive mother's relatives; at least, she wanted to be too, since they were her only 'family' to her. In fact, as she was growing up, there was no hint whatsoever from any of the extended kin of her adoptive mother that she was a non-Indian. That Jane was Chinese was an idea that was completely muted.

Once in school—it might have been in 1948—the nuns insisted Jane indicate her ethnicity as Chinese in a form that all the students were asked to complete. After that incident in school that day, Jane recalled running home in a frenzy as she wanted to check the veracity of the information she had received about her identity. Until this day, she remembers the response from her adoptive mother: 'Don't worry about what they say. You are fair because, when you were a baby, you fell into a pot of milk!' At a tender young age, Jane, in her naïvety, believed every word her adoptive mother said. But as she grew older, it became increasingly obvious to her that she probably was not the Indian girl she had thought herself to be. It was a gradual epiphany, not a distinct event, that brought on this realization of who she really was. It ended in her eventually realizing to the fact that she might have been adopted.

It was also in Seremban in 1950 that her adoptive mother signed the bond linked to the Child and Youth Ordinance Young Persons Ordinance, 1948 [Section 17(3) Form VIII] since she was never legally adopted. Signing the bond meant that Jane's adoptive mother vowed never to put her 'adopted' daughter into prostitution or any other vice activities. The bond also signified that her adoptive mother had taken an oath never to give Jane to the 'care, custody, or control' of anyone else as long as she was under the age of eighteen! If she did, she would be liable to pay a fine of 200 SGD to the colonial government. But like her baptismal certificate, the document was crucial for one key reason: it affirmed the relationship between her adoptive mother and herself and noted that the relationship was one of adoption and not of blood.

While it is unclear what events led to Jane's adoptive mother signing the document, that action clarified a few things. Jane's adoption had been informal otherwise known as a de facto adoption. In fact, most 'adoptions' were de facto until the 1960s in spite of the Adoption Ordinance of 1939, and these children were vulnerable to being abused in various ways. In many countries, there are laws and institutions to protect children and to ensure their safety. This is tied to the fact that children, unlike adults, are vulnerable to being exploited, abused, or neglected. That children are especially at risk in society compared to adults has been recognized by the state. That is why we have the United Nations Convention of the Rights of the Child (UNCRC)—the assumption being children deserve special care and protection because of their physical and mental immaturity. Children can also face abuse at the hands of those whom they might believe to be trustworthy.

Throughout Singapore's history, there have been many instances in which children were exploited or suffered immeasurable harm. It must be remembered that this was a time during which a girl child could be transferred to become a servant in someone's household, a practice which the colonial government viewed as a social problem. These girls were called '*mui tsai*', '*mui*' meaning 'younger sister' and '*tsai*' meaning 'little' in Cantonese, although the phrase is actually understood as 'little servant girl'. This was also a time in which girls or young women were forced into prostitution against their will. Because of the vulnerability of children and youth, the British enacted several ordinances with the aim of protecting children and young people. The Children's Ordinance was only one. The other was the Child and Youth Ordinance Young Persons Ordinance of 1948. It must be remembered that those were times marked by poverty and economic disadvantage—conditions ripe for child maltreatment.

To Singapore

Because she struggled to find work in Malaya in that atmosphere of crisis, Jane's adoptive mother decided to move to Singapore. It was at the advice of a good friend, Mr Tambiya Naidu, that her adoptive mother applied for a job in Singapore in 1949 at the KK Women's and Children's Hospital. Her adoptive mother made the move to Singapore in 1950; Jane followed in 1951.

On arriving in Singapore in 1951, Jane remembers attending St Teresa's Convent for the first three months. Located along Tiong Bahru Road, the school did not have a proper building and resembled a shed. As midwives and nurses had to live in the hospital quarters, Jane was soon transferred to the Convent of the Holy Infant Jesus (CHIJ), Victoria Street, where she was a 'second-class boarder' at the convent for two years. Packing Jane off to the convent as a boarder proved to be much easier for her adoptive mother, who could concentrate on the demands of her new job: working on continuous morning and afternoon shifts, followed by two weeks of night duty. Moreover, off days were scarce, making it very difficult for her adoptive mother to juggle both her work and taking proper care of Jane.

As Jane recalls, life was regimented as a boarder in the convent. There were specific times for prayers, morning Mass in the chapel, and then there were the daily chores each boarder had to undertake. Not that Jane was unaccustomed to any form of discipline, but her greatest worry was that all this meant that she was left with less time to study. Her favourite subjects were Science and Latin. She attributes her love for these subjects to the teachers she had—an Irish nun named Sister Elizabeth, who taught her Science, while Latin was taught by Sister Cecile. So, she had to be mindful about completing her chores on time.

For her adoptive mother, the separation from Jane was painful but necessary for that short while. Making only eighty Singapore dollars a month at that time, thirty-five Singapore dollars—which was a tidy sum of her monthly earnings—was channelled to keep Jane in the convent boarding school! This was the cost of being a second-class boarder, so one can imagine how much it would have cost to have a daughter stay as a first-class boarder. Although a child, Jane was quick to observe that the nuns treated the second-class boarders a little differently from the first-class boarders— they ended up doing more chores like sweeping the staircase, and the nuns seemed to be much stricter with them if they did not complete those chores on time. But there were good things that came out of the experience of staying in the convent as a boarder. She always looked forward to attending Sunday mass at the Cathedral of the Good Shepherd at which all the boarders had to wear a white blouse, brown pinafore, and a hat. Having been a boarder, Jane feels the experience instilled in her the ability to be neat and organized with her possessions. The two years Jane stayed in the convent flew by very quickly.

Soon her adoptive mother found a very large rented room in a building located across the KK Hospital. After this, Jane was never to be separated from her again. On days when her adoptive mother was on night duty, she remembers going to stay overnight with the Joseph family since her adoptive mother was fearful of leaving Jane alone in the room they had rented. Mrs Arul Marie Joseph was a close friend of her adoptive mother. She had met her in Seremban in the late 1940s. When they met, Arul Marie was unmarried. In 1952, on marrying Mr Selvaraju Joseph at the age of twenty-five, she found herself moving to Singapore to join her husband. As he worked in the Malayan Railways, the family lived in the railway quarters at Spooner Road, not too far from where Jane and her adoptive mother lived. So, it was not difficult to drop Jane off at the home of the Joseph family for a day when the need arose.

The relationship between Jane's adoptive mother and Arul Marie went beyond being good friends. Jane's adoptive mother would end up delivering Arul Marie's first child. It was July 1955. Having had two miscarriages, Arul Marie was reluctant to go to the hospital, fearing that she could lose the child she was carrying. Aware that Arul Marie was having labour pains and unsuccessful in convincing her to go to the hospital, Jane's adoptive mother, who was visiting Arul Marie at that time, sprang into action with the assistance of the neighbour. The story goes that she delivered the child using a pair of sewing scissors to cut the umbilical cord. The placenta was later buried in the garden behind their home across the 'running bungalow', where the train drivers used to stay before taking the next train back to Johor. The 'running bungalow' still stands to this day.

The following year, 1957, was the next milestone in Jane's life. She completed her Senior Cambridge or GCE O-Level. Although she did well in her studies, she failed to make the grade to enter medical school at the local university. So, she trained instead to become a teacher at the behest of her adoptive mother, who did not want her to pursue a career in nursing, considering it to be a 'dirty' and 'tough' job. Instead, Jane's adoptive mother wanted her to become a teacher. In those days, a person who was a teacher was held in high regard. The teaching profession was considered a respectable one.

But Jane was faced with a formidable hurdle in getting a teaching job. She did not have a birth certificate! It was then that her adoptive mother's good friend by the name of Gertrude Lee, whom Jane's adoptive mother had met in the convent in Seremban, played a key role in helping Jane. She had also migrated to Singapore and was working at the supermarket at the Navy, Army and Air Force Institutes (NAAFI), Britannia, a British club located along Beach Road, before becoming a midwife herself on the advice of Jane's adoptive mother. It was Aunty Gertrude who eventually helped her secure a Statutory Declaration in March 1957. The Statutory Declaration was a critical document, just like her baptism certificate and the bond linked to the Child and Youth Ordinance Young Persons Ordinance, 1948 [Section 17(3) Form VIII], which her adoptive mother had signed. It was a formal document revealing the relationship Jane's adoptive mother had with her, primarily her role as Jane's guardian. But, in contrast to the other two documents, the declaration contained Jane's date of birth and her place of birth, as well as the year in which she had been baptized. It was a legal document signed under oath.

Marriage, home, and work

Soon after entering the Teacher's Training College (TTC) in 1957, Jane was married in 1960 at the Church of the Immaculate Heart of Mary, along Highland Road, off Upper Serangoon Road. For the church wedding, Jane wore a white silk saree since the family was Christian. It was a long, drawn out affair, stretching over three days, as was common in those days. On the first day, her adoptive mother, Mrs Joseph, welcomed her colleagues from the hospital to her home and served high tea. In a celebratory fashion, guests danced to music. On the second day, a restaurant reception was held for the groom's 'band boys' called the Blue Harmonics. On the actual day of the wedding, a tea reception was held at the Indian Association along Balestier Road. Extended family from Malaysia, close friends in Singapore, and colleagues from Balestier Girls' School in Singapore, where Jane taught, attended the wedding celebration. Being Christian, she had a tiered wedding cake. It was a fruitcake, lavishly decorated with royal icing.

Her husband, Wilson Devasahayam, was a teacher by vocation who taught English and music in school. He was a relative of her adoptive mother and had moved to Singapore in search of work around the same time Jane and her adoptive mother had arrived. It was an arranged marriage as many Indian marriages were in the past. After her marriage, she took on her husband's surname but was called Mrs Wilson as it was easier for everyone to pronounce and remember.

Jane's home life could be described as mostly 'Indian'. Jane continued to speak both Tamil and English in her matrimonial home. With her adoptive mother, who lived with her for a few

years to help look after her four children, Jane spoke mainly
Tamil. With her husband, and later her children, she spoke in
English, although they were able to comprehend some Tamil.
Moreover, Jane regularly enjoyed watching Tamil movies at home
and could identify the Tamil actors and actresses who were 'stars'
and captured the hearts of many in the 1950s and 1960s. Her
favourites were Gemini Ganesan and Savitri, both of whom Jane
found stunning.

In terms of the food the family ate at home, it was mostly South
Indian cuisine, although, on occasion, local fare such as *mee goreng*
or *kway teow* was prepared. Christmastime was the exception.
British brandied fruitcake was baked without fail every year,
usually in the month of August, and stored in air-tight Huntley
& Palmers biscuit tins to be cured until Christmas. Christmas was
the only religious festival the family celebrated. Occasionally, the
family celebrated Easter, but it was a smallish affair and not on the
scale Christmas would have been celebrated each year with family
and close family friends. Another habit that could be considered
'Western', possibly because she was raised a Christian, was Jane's
taste in music. While the family listened to mainly Western music
such as jazz or songs from the easy listening genre characteristic of
the 1950s, years into her marriage, she took an interest in playing
classical piano, especially since her husband played the piano as
well. At his coaxing, she eventually decided to pursue her desire to
play the piano by taking lessons at the Far Eastern Music School,
located in the Dhoby Ghaut area. It was run by the famed Asciano
family, who were Spanish Filipino. Even today, if she is asked what
her favourite tunes are, they will be 'La Paloma' and 'Danny Boy'.

Who am I?

In June 1973, the family made a trip to West Malaysia. They did
this fairly frequently during the school holidays to visit relatives.
Cramped into the family's sky-blue Ford Anglia car were Jane, her

adoptive mother, and three children, as her fourth was yet to be born, while her husband was behind the wheel. A quick stopover was made in Kulai, Johor, as Jane's adoptive mother was curious if the house she had been to the day she went to receive Jane as an infant was still standing. Alas, the entire physical landscape of the town had drastically transformed. The family asked some shopkeepers if they knew of a farmer who owned a chicken and pig farm in the area. But no one knew anything of significance. Jane's fate was sealed. From then on, she was never going to know her 'Chinese' roots. Many years later, when the topic of her biological family came up, she would speak openly about being fortunate to have been adopted into the family she did. She said she was happy to have been raised an 'Indian', the community of which she considers herself a part till today.

Although feeling 'Indian' in many ways, Jane found it difficult to deny her Chinese identity, an enduring point of certainty, mostly because of her physical appearance. When she went out and a stranger in the street asked for directions in Chinese, she usually responded politely by letting the person know that she could not speak Chinese. In fact, this happened quite frequently as there was no semblance of anything Indian in her dress code—in her adulthood, Jane always wore Western clothing, usually a dress, if not a blouse and a pair of pants, and did not wear any Indian-style jewellery or a *pottu* on her forehead. Only if she attended an Indian wedding did she wear a saree. Invariably, these strangers, whom she would encounter in public, would be perplexed on learning that Jane could not speak any Chinese—it was the norm for the Chinese people of her generation to speak at least one Chinese dialect. However, in Little India, the response she received was in stark contrast to this. Whenever she spoke in Tamil to the shopkeepers or salesgirls, it seemed like they instinctively knew that Jane was adopted into an Indian family and so spoke Tamil fluently. In fact, nobody seemed surprised at how fluent she was in the language!

Even amongst her colleagues, many quickly figured out that she spoke Tamil as she had been adopted. In the schools she taught, she forged friendships with all the teachers regardless of their racial or religious background. At Paya Lebar Methodist Primary School, where Jane taught for ten years, she had a particular fondness for a young teacher who was Tamil. Their friendship developed over the years since they both spoke the Tamil language and shared cultural commonalities. As to the rest of the teachers whom she worked with—whether they were Chinese or Eurasian—she continued to stay in touch with them even after her retirement at the age of fifty-eight. In fact, she always spoke of how immensely she profited from her friendships with her Chinese colleagues. It was through them that Jane learned how some traditional Chinese medicines worked just as well as, or even better than, Western allopathic treatments. But, invariably, her closest friends were mostly Indian, with the exception of the Tan family, whom her family as well as her adoptive mother had known for more than sixty years as they were Gertrude's closest kin in Singapore.

But there was no denying the fact that she felt most comfortable amongst her adoptive Indian relatives and friends, having been raised in an Indian family. This is in spite of some distant relatives referring to her as the 'Chinese girl' whom her adoptive mother had taken in and raised. Her being labelled as the adoptive 'Chinese girl' came up during the passing of her adoptive brother in Kuala Lumpur in October 2022. As slides of her adoptive brother were flashed on the wall in the St Francis Xavier's Church in memory of significant milestones of his life, Jane appeared in several of them. In those slides, standing in a sea of Indian faces, was this Chinese-looking young woman, as if an outsider to the family, although in reality, she was very much a part of the family, especially to her closest adoptive kin.

How she felt about her identity is far more complex than what was apparent. If she was openly asked about her identity, she never

denied her 'Indian' affiliation. And if she was forced to choose
one ethnic group over another and had to use a label to describe
herself, she never doubted the fact that she was 'Indian', having
been raised in an Indian family. In spite of looking Chinese and
adopting some Western habits, Jane is in many ways an 'Indian'
woman at heart. And this could not have been possible without a
·loving set of adoptive parents, who had been complete strangers
to her at birth.

With Jane's mother Grace Imelda Joseph;
photo taken in Seremban, Malaysia in 1947.

Jane's mother and Gertrude Lee were the best of friends. Because Jane did not have a birth certificate, it was Auntie Gertrude who helped Jane secure the relevant documents she needed to apply for a job as a teacher.

A studio photo taken in 1954 of Jane and Maggie Nathan, the daughter of Jane's adoptive mother's good friend Collette Nathan. Jane's adoptive mother and Collette met through the convent and developed a friendship that would last for many decades.

With her mother; photo taken in 1960 before Jane got married.

*Jane and her adoptive mother, Grace, her adoptive brother, Anthony, and his wife,
Josephine, and their son, Julian; together with her two daughters, Patricia (next
to her) and Theresa (the author of the book, standing to the left of Jane's adoptive
mother). This studio picture was taken around 1966.*

Jane with her daughter Theresa W. Devasahayam, the author of this book.

Chapter 12

Happy to Be Adopted

Finding a good home

It was a rainy night in 1960. At the front gate of the home of James Arathoon Martin Sarkies was a young woman, carrying an infant swaddled in a blanket. In the pouring rain, the gate swung open, and she was immediately motioned to come inside the house. Walking hurriedly to the main door, she encountered Mae Didier, wife of James Sarkies. The young woman soon started to beg Mae Didier to take her daughter.

This young woman probably heard from others in the neighbourhood that the couple had recently adopted a baby girl and decided to try her luck to see if James Sarkies and his wife would take in another child. James Sarkies and his wife were an older couple. He was fifty years old at that time, and Mae was forty years old. They already had two children of their own— Loretta and Jessie.

Susan was the seventh child in her biological family, and it was impossible for her birth parents to keep her as they were very poor. As they could not raise another child, they had only one choice: to find the child a good home where she will be raised and well provided for. As soon as Loretta, who was to become Susan's oldest adoptive sister, set her eyes on Susan as a baby in her mother's arms, she cajoled her mother to take the child in, instantly falling in love with the infant. Years later, Susan was to learn that Loretta was drawn to her because of her beautiful, curly black hair. A young woman herself of around twenty years of age, Loretta quickly thought that Susan would be the perfect playmate for Ruby, whom James Sarkies and his wife had adopted a few months earlier. Ruby and Susan were around the same age. Such was the start of Susan's journey as the second adopted child in the Sarkies family. That evening would lead inexorably to her adoption.

A formal adoption

Susan Sarkies was a few weeks old when she was adopted into the Sarkies family. Unlike other 'adoptions' that took place in pre-independence Singapore, Susan's adoption was formal. Her adoptive parents had sought the services of a lawyer to have her formally received into the family. As a result, her birth certificate reflected the names of her adoptive parents, James Sarkies and Mae Didier. Her case was in contrast to the many adoptions occurring during the years leading up to the 1960s. Up until the early 1960s, in pre-independence Singapore, most adoptions tended to be de facto. In other words, they were not accompanied by any legal documentation, which meant that these children, who considered themselves to be 'adopted', were technically not adopted but 'transferred'. As formally adopting a child meant incurring legal fees, it might not have been possible for many adoptive couples during those times. They could not have afforded to take the legal route for receiving the children they wished to raise.

As Susan was legally adopted, there was just one detail in her birth certificate which was revealing: the place of her birth. There it was stated that she was born at 737 Poh Huat Road, suggesting that her birth parents lived in the same *kampong* as her adoptive parents in the Upper Serangoon Road area. That the birth certificate had that one trace of Susan's origins meant that Susan could, if she wanted to, go in search of her biological relatives.

While it had crossed her mind in the past to seek them out, her desire to locate her biological family waned as she got married and started a family of her own. Also, her adoptive parents did not keep in touch with her biological parents as they did not know each other. The fact that there was no 'prior relationship' between the families meant that it did not make any sense for her to seek out her birth relatives.

Susan might have been around ten or eleven years of age when she discovered her adoption papers and became more aware about her adoption. But it was not as if she had been clueless about her adoption before that. She had an inkling that she was adopted since she did not look anything like her adoptive parents and siblings. When the family sold the house to move to Toa Payoh, a drawer was being emptied. From within it emerged her adoption papers, together with other documents—her baptism and confirmation certificates. It was then that the fact of her adoption was confirmed. On discovering this truth, Susan felt a surge of mixed emotions. But she never responded negatively to her adoption. Instead, she chose to let the matter go. For her, pursuing the matter seemed to be worthless as she 'did not want to bring the past back', neither did she feel the need to unearth her past. She could only think of the 'good things' she received from the Sarkies family. She 'was very happy with the life' she had led till then. In fact, the truth is that many adopted children tended to get more opportunities than children who were raised by their biological family, and Susan's case reflected that reality.

Her upbringing

It is inevitable that Susan drew this conclusion about her adoption, especially since she was adopted into a family that was fairly well-to-do. As a boy, James Sarkies had attended the prestigious Raffles' Institution and made a life for himself. After getting married, he worked for several car companies as a manager, first in Fiat

Company, then Wearns Used Carmart; and lastly, in Singapore Motors, which was located smack in the middle of Orchard Road. Trips to his office on occasions meant Susan having her favourite peach melba ice-cream at the Magnolia House near Fitzpatrick Supermarket! As a manager in those days, he received a monthly salary to the tune of 700 SGD. With a handsome salary, he could provide a fairly luxurious lifestyle for his wife and children.

Considered fairly well-off, the family lived in a bungalow along Da Silva Lane off Upper Serangoon Road. Sometime around 1954–1955, it was purchased for 12,000 SGD. The house sat on an acre of land! It would be considered a large house by the standards of that day since it had six bedrooms and a garage for three cars. It also had a large garden area in which sat an aviary for pigeons. Susan recalled that everyone in the family loved animals. Their pets extended to dogs, cats, geese, chicken, rabbits, and even a turkey! The house was also made of concrete. This was unlike the other houses in the area, with the exception of a house owned by a medical doctor a few doors away. Generally, the houses were poorly built and constructed mainly out of wood.

In those days, European families in Singapore had an entourage of servants—maids, cooks, drivers, nannies, gardeners, and so forth. The Sarkies family, although Armenian, was no different. They had two Chinese servants who came in every day to help with the household chores, each receiving a monthly salary of around $10. The family also had drivers, and so Susan and her sisters found themselves being chauffeured everywhere they needed to go. But the Sarkies' family was down-to-earth at the same time in spite of enjoying the luxuries of an upper-middle class lifestyle. Susan and Ruby travelled to school by 'school bus'. This meant that they had to be punctual in the morning while going to school, unlike if they had one of their drivers ferry them. Susan and Ruby, as well as Loretta and Jessie, attended first Punggol Convent and then St Joseph's Convent, both not very far from home and were classmates for ten years! Susan also fondly remembers the corner coffeeshop at the junction of Upper Serangoon Road and Simon Road. There was a food stall owner who served an excellent *chah ta kueh* or stir-fried rice flour cake. It was a savoury dish made from rice flour and radish, laced with garlic, onion, fish sauce, and chili sauce, and she thought it was 'to die for!' An interesting fact that she recalls from those days was that if customers wanted to have the dish with egg, they had to bring the egg along with them to be cooked with the other ingredients.

The reputation of the Sarkies' family was to go beyond that upper middle-class lifestyle. James Sarkies was from a prominent and wealthy family in Southeast Asia. The Sarkies were known for being hotel magnates, constructing luxury hotels in the region. One of the three granduncles of James Sarkies had built the famous colonial-style luxury Raffles Hotel in Singapore in 1887 while another granduncle was responsible for establishing Adelphi Hotel, another principal hotel in Singapore in the late nineteenth century together with Raffles Hotel, Hotel de l'Europe, and Hotel de la Paix. The last of the Sarkies brothers, of the three granduncles of James Sarkies, went offshore and established the colonial-style hotel, the Eastern & Oriental Hotel in Georgetown, Penang, in 1889. In Singapore, their fame led to a road being named after the family along Bukit Timah Road.

The wealth of the Armenian community appeared to know no bounds. Under the British Raj, the Armenians were amongst the first merchants to arrive in Singapore. Despite their small numbers, they played a significant role in the economic life of Singapore. Some of the early settlers amongst the community owned factories, others worked in banks. In the region, some Armenian families owned stone or diamond factories, which was the case amongst the Armenians living in Thailand. Because there was a limited number of Armenian companies in Singapore the

1960s and 1970s, James Sarkies decided not to seek employment within the Armenian community. Besides, he had very few Armenian friends and was not close to the Armenian community.

To say that the Sarkies family was a family of means was an understatement for another reason. Birthday celebrations for James Sarkies at 8 Da Silva Lane were a lavish affair, and he would have one every year. Born on New Year's Day, the celebration included good food and music and friends coming over. Susan remembers how the garden and driveway would be decorated with lanterns, adding to the celebratory mood of the evening. To top it all, there was a mini fireworks display. Thus, it was no ordinary birthday party. 'It was grand and loud', to say the least.

For most of her childhood, Susan remembers her adoptive father to be a very quiet, patient, and kind man. She never saw him lose his temper. He was also known to be a generous person, always willing to help others in times of need. Of her adoptive parents, her mother was the disciplinarian. It was she who held formidable power in the family. Susan was James' favourite daughter while Ruby was doted on by their adoptive mother. Her adoptive sisters, Loretta and Jessie, as Susan recalls, always treated Susan and Ruby as their siblings. They looked out for their adoptive sisters, and never once did they treat them any less well than biological sisters would.

Family matters were left in the hands of Mae Sarkies, who made most of the major decisions concerning the household. She did the grocery shopping, cared for the pets, took charge of the servants, and maintained the household within the budget given to her by her husband. But that did not mean James Sarkies did not play an active part in raising his daughters. He often spent time at home, when he was not at work. Susan recalls vividly the car rides the family took. While James Sarkies would be at the wheel with Mae next to him, Susan, Ruby, and Loretta's children,

Brigitte and Carol, were forced to cramp themselves in the back seat. One of the games they played during car rides was 'guess the car'. Susan found this to be challenging, especially as the different models of cars whizzed past them, some travelling at breakneck speed, and it was near impossible trying to pin down their make.

It was in 1973 that Susan's adoptive sister Jessie met a ballet teacher by the name of Lorraine. Jessie would play the piano in Lorraine's ballet classes. It was there that Susan took a fertile interest in ballet and eventually become a ballet teacher herself, completing all the grades for the Royal Academy of Dance (London). Along the way, Ruby started helping another ballet teacher as well. After completing her O-levels, Susan decided to work as an assistant ballet teacher at the British Association of Singapore Ballet School. She was seventeen years of age at that time. It was also during this time that Susan's love for the performing arts flourished. She was then with the music and drama group—The Sceneshifters—at the YMCA, together with Jessie, Ruby, and the man whom she would eventually marry.

Her marriage

At the age of sixteen, at a New Year's Eve party in 1976, Susan met her husband-to-be, Gerry, through her niece's boyfriend. It was love at first sight and love blossomed very quickly. The performing arts was the glue that brought them together. They were both cast in the musicals *Fiddler on the Roof* and *Flower Drum Song*. He was there during the saddest period of her life—on the passing of James Sarkies in 1977, aged sixty-nine. Susan was seventeen years old. Gerry helped with the funeral arrangements and was there to comfort Susan, her mother, and her sisters. On marrying Gerry in 1981 at twenty-one years of age, she decided to take his last name—Cheong, appending it to her own name. Thus, today, she goes by the name Susan Cheong Sarkies.

Gerry was of Hakka stock. Not knowing anything about Chinese culture in spite of looking Chinese—even her identity card states that she is Armenian by ethnicity—Susan has adapted well to the family she married into, enjoying Chinese New Year reunions with her husband's relatives. She also learned how to speak a smattering of Hakka in order to communicate with her mother-in-law. With her father-in-law, she spoke Malay, the language she took as her second language in school. Even the food she had grown up eating was less Chinese and more Eurasian, as the family ate devil's curry, shepherd's pie, brandied fruitcake, and Russian salad, and, thus, she had to make some adjustments in her marriage. In spite of the cultural differences, Susan has had a wonderful marriage and three beautiful children—Darin, Brendan, and Megan.

Unlike James Sarkies, Mae Didier lived a fairly long life, passing on in 2006 at the age of eighty-six. A few years later, in 2013, Susan was eventually to lose Jessie, who fought a battle against cancer. Till today, she misses both of them dearly.

The Sarkies name

The name Sarkies has become embedded in the history books of Singapore because of Susan's adoptive father's uncles and the legacy they left in the hotels they built in Singapore and the region. For some years, Susan had been contemplating renaming her dance school 'Forms Ballet and Dance Centre' to 'Sarkies School of Dance'. The school could have been the avenue through which she could keep the Sarkies name alive. But she laments how age is catching up with her and that there is no successor interested in continuing the business of running the dance school. So, she has had to cast that idea aside.

Affirming her Armenian heritage

The Armenians are a tight-knit ethnic group in Singapore, even though their community is small. It has even been dwindling over the decades, with many families migrating to Australia over time.

Yet they have a church of their own standing along Armenian Street—the Armenian Apostolic Church of St Gregory the Illuminator. Other than church services, the Coptic Orthodox Church has been the focal point of activities for the Armenians in Singapore, hosting barbecues, and chess tournaments and organizing Armenian music events. Concerts have been held at the church since the church could seat around 100 people.

But James Sarkies and his wife, unlike most Armenians in Singapore, were Roman Catholics. This might have been because Mae was of French-Filipino descent. Because of their Roman Catholic affiliation, it was fitting that the Sarkies daughters attended Convent schools. In school, Susan remembers being asked often as to why she was carrying the name Sarkies. In order to stop her classmates from asking anymore questions, she would directly tell them that she was adopted—a fact that she would never hide. Eventually, everyone knew that Susan and Ruby were adoptive sisters. Separated by only two days in age, they came to be known as the 'Sarkies unidentical twins'.

Even today, some people mistakenly believe that she married an Armenian by the name of Sarkies and thus took on the name through marriage. In reality, however, Susan is a Sarkies herself, albeit through adoption. Although she is not close to members of the Armenian community in Singapore, if she does attend any of their gatherings, her response to their question—should anyone in the community inquire about her Armenian status—would always be the same. She would tell them that she was one of the adopted daughters of James Sarkies. The same applied to her ballet students. She has retained the name Sarkies and has never concealed the fact of her adoption. In reacting to her adoption, Susan has always been pleased that there was 'someone who wanted her', expressing her eternal gratitude to her adoptive parents. For her, 'from childhood to this present day', she has only taken pride in being a member of the Sarkies family. She has only happy memories about her adoption.

Ruby and Susan aged seven years at 8 Da Silva Lane.

The two adopted Sarkies daughters, Ruby and Susan, as teenagers.

A family outing at Sentosa in 1978 with Mummy Mae, Ruby, Jessie, and Susan.

Chapter 13

The Hospital Connection

Singapore's premier maternity hospital

Thanaletchmi Varatharaaju was adopted by an Indian couple through a contact her adoptive mother had in the hospital. Growing up, her adoption was not spoken about in great detail, and she never saw the need to probe. But she had a sense that it was through a hospital *amah* that she came to be adopted. Her presupposition was fuelled by the fact that her adoptive mother's friend who worked as an *amah* in the Kandang Kerbau Hospital had also adopted a Chinese girl. The girl, however, was a year older than Thanaletchmi.

Hospitals were the place where children were born, and it was at hospitals that children were also adopted, Thanaletchmi surmised. In the past, hospital adoptions took place in Singapore. It was not that the hospital became involved as a formal go-between between an adoptive couple and the biological parents of a child, but if a woman did not want to keep her child, hospital staff could have stepped in to help spread the word that a child was available for adoption.

It was in 1966 that Thanaletchmi was born—the year in which Kandang Kerbau Hospital made it to the Guinness Book of Records for having had the highest number of births amongst all the hospitals in the world—39,835 to be exact! (Various other figures for the hospital birth rate have been put forward but they all above 39,000). It is not known, however, what had led to the explosion of births. Could it be a continuation of the baby boom? Or could it have been the separation of Singapore from Malaysia in 1965 that caused many from the peninsula to move to Singapore, seeking jobs and a permanent residence, and so the island saw a boost in its population because of an influx of foreigners?

Prior to the 1940s, being a mother-to-be was a perilous experience. It was a known occurrence that sometimes the mother died in childbirth, or the child did not survive. It was only logical for many women to choose to have the baby in the hospital rather than at home, given that expectant mothers would receive the immediate specialist care they needed, averting unnecessary deaths. As hospital births gained popularity from the late 1940s, the numbers of infants born in a hospital gradually increased over time. In those days, only the Malays continued to choose a home birth, calling in a *bidan*—traditional birth attendant—to assist the mother-to-be in the birthing process. The majority of women in Singapore—especially amongst the Chinese and Indians— chose a hospital birth over a home birth.

In the 1950s and the years that followed, hospital births became the norm in Singapore. Kandang Kerbau Hospital, otherwise known as KK Hospital, was where most infants were born. The name Kandang Kerbau in Malay could be literally translated as 'buffalo pen'. It was said that it got its name because the hospital was located near a buffalo shed. Eventually, even the acronym KK was used in place of KK Hospital. Initially established as a general hospital in 1858, KK Hospital was converted into a maternity hospital in 1924 to serve a growing population. In 1950, there were slightly less than 1,000 babies being born there each month. The years 1956 and 1957 saw a stunning rise of 25,000 and 29,000 births, respectively: double that of the deliveries in 1951. The numbers continued to increase until 1970, when births dropped below 30,000. Aside from being in the business of childbirth and saving lives, the hospital was unique in one respect: it was devoted to teaching obstetrics and gynaecology to medical students and training midwives.

The hospital hired a range of staff to ensure that the healthcare services provided to patients would run smoothly. At one end of the spectrum were what was called the *amahs*. Instantly recognizable in the hospital setting, all the female Indian *amahs* wore a blouse and a long skirt, unlike the Chinese *amahs*, who would wear a blouse and a pair of pants. There were also men who were hired for the job. Hospital *amahs* carried out the most mundane, but nonetheless important, tasks. They wheel-chaired patients who came in, delivered patient files to doctors and nurses, and delivered meals to patients.

Such was the job of Thanaletchmi's adoptive mother's friend, who would eventually become her godmother when Thanaletchmi came of age. Her family as well as Thanaletchmi's adoptive parents lived in the rented flats along Race Course Road at that time. The area had already grown to be a haunt of Indian immigrants, eventually becoming known as Little India. The Race Course flats were not far from KK Hospital. It was a short walk away. Many hospital staff stayed in the area for the simple reason that commuting to work would be much easier. It was in 1954 that Thanaletchmi's parents moved into one of those flats, and they stayed there for many years. The community was close-knit. Thanaletchmi's parents made many friends with the other families living in the flats, and the families looked out for one another, to the extent of helping each other in times of need. Those were the days when people would visit or share sweetmeats with one another during celebrations or festivals.

Moment of awakening

Growing up, Thanaletchmi did not have much information about her adoption. And the idea of 'being an adopted child' never crossed her mind. Although her adoptive parents, who hailed from south India, were different in appearance from her, she recalls not being even conscious of this fact. As she lived in a racially diverse neighbourhood, she felt that, in those days, nobody seemed to bother about 'race' or wondered why she looked very different from her 'parents'. As for the Indian families in the neighbourhood, she did not think any of them saw her as Chinese.

That said, the pivotal moment in her life came when she was twelve. That was when she saw her birth certificate for the first time since she needed the document to secure her identity card (IC). Accompanied by her father to an office at Empress Place to get this done, she had a rude shock on discovering that her adoptive parents' names were not documented in her birth certificate. Rather, staring at her were the names of Chinese individuals whom she did not know. While she admits that she was upset on discovering about her adoption, she eventually came to accept it, not allowing it to bother her too much.

For Thanaletchmi, her adoptive parents were her 'real' parents. As she was growing up, she was the only daughter they had, although they had lost a child of their own in infancy. This child was born in 1961 or 1962, and would have been four or five years older than her, had it survived. A fact of her adoption was that her adoptive parents were an elderly couple when they received her—her adoptive father might have been around fifty-five years of age at that time. She knows this for a fact since, when she turned eighteen or nineteen, he was seventy-five years old! While her adoptive father was a carpenter, her adoptive mother was a homemaker.

After coming to realize that she was adopted when she was twelve, only once did she inquire of her adoptive parents about that.

She might have been in her late teens when she broached the subject with her adoptive mother. The only thing she learned was that she was the eighth child in the family, and, probably, her parents could not keep her because they had too many children.

It was not uncommon for adoptive parents to actively hide the child's adoption in the hope that the child would never find out the 'truth' surrounding the adoption. And if the child ever broached the topic, this was quickly dismissed as if it were a non-question. This was the experience of Thanaletchmi too. Because she could sense that her adoptive mother did not want to reveal more about her adoption, she let the matter drop. But this only occurred amongst adoptees who did not know their birth parents. There was a large number of such children.

Although Thanaletchmi knew her adoptive mother had more information about her biological family, never once did she entertain the thought of seeking them out. She could have done that since the address of her biological parents was written in her birth certificate. Instead, she heartily quips that her lackadaisical attitude towards her biological relatives stems from the fact that 'she is happy where she is', and there is no need to pursue the matter. Neither is she curious about the reasons she was given away, rationalizing that knowing more is 'not going to help her in anyway'. And if she ever changes her mind and does locate them, she will have an even bigger family than she already has at present—something she does not desire. Hence, she is quite content to leave the matter of her adoption in the past.

Marriage, family, and work

Thanaletchmi recalls her childhood was a fairly happy one. Her adoptive parents took good care of her, gave her an education, and eventually agreed to her marriage at the age of twenty-two. She married a man who grew up in the same neighbourhood. She would see his older brother playing football at the

Farrer Park soccer field near the rental flats several times a week with his friends. He caught her attention only because he was a twin, and, thus, stood out from the other men. At that time, she did not know him or his family, let alone his youngest brother, whom she would eventually marry. But fate would have it that the older brother was the matchmaker for Thanaletchmi and her husband-to-be. Their acquaintance was only made when the offer of a marriage proposal came. This prompted her adoptive parents to agree to the marriage since Thanaletchmi was of marriageable age.

Arrangements were made, and the day for the wedding was picked. But unlike many Hindu marriages in which the astrologer was consulted to ascertain if the couple were a good match, in the case of Thanaletchmi and her husband, nothing like that was done. Although drawing the admonition of her husband-to-be's eldest brother, who acted as the matchmaker in their union, her husband-to-be insisted on going ahead with the wedding as he had taken a liking for her, having seen her around in the neighbourhood many times.

Thanaletchmi works as a bank manager today and has two wonderful daughters whom she dotes on. Interestingly enough, the mother of the man whom she married is also an adopted child. But unlike Thanaletchmi, her husband's mother was either abandoned or got separated from her birth family during the Japanese occupation. This was not unheard of, especially since families had been displaced with some losing their lives, leaving their children to fend for themselves. When families in the *kampong* along St George's Road could not locate her parents, Thanaletchmi's husband's grandparents swiftly took her in, raised her, and later married her off to their eldest son. She was a teenager then, around thirteen or fourteen years of age. Her adoptive parents were prompted to take her in, as being Chinese could have put her at risk of being targeted by the Japanese. The family now surmises that it could have been possible that her own parents were killed by the Japanese. Adopting a girl with the express purpose of having her married to a son in the family was not uncommon, although this practice was more prevalent amongst the Chinese than the Indians. That being said, raising others' children was fairly common in those days. As it was also common for people to look out for each other, leading to several forms of child adoption, like in the case of Thanaletchmi's mother-in-law.

Every way an Indian

Because her adoptive parents were Indian, more specifically Tamil, her upbringing was Indian in every possible way. She grew up speaking Tamil, eating Indian food, and watching Indian movies. There is not a trace of Chineseness in her except for her appearance. It was only in school—to be precise, Rangoon Secondary School, where she did her GCE O-Level—that Thanaletchmi became conscious of her racial identity. An enthusiastic long-distance runner, she left her classmates and teachers astonished that a Chinese could have won the first prize: a blatant racial stereotype of what the Chinese could accomplish as it was assumed that only the Indians could excel in the sport.

Today, Thanaletchmi is comfortable with calling herself an 'Indian'. When she dresses up for the office every day, without fail she applies a *pottu*—decorative mark—on her forehead, even if she is attired in a Western dress like a blouse and a pair of pants. Using a *pottu* on her forehead comes naturally to her as she feels 'complete' with it. She does not see this as going out of her way to display her south Indian identity.

Once outside her home, however, she finds it bemusing that there are Chinese who assume that she is Chinese. Typically, they come up to her and speak with her in Mandarin. Most of these individuals, she says, tend to be fairly young, and, thus, one would expect them to communicate with her in English rather than Chinese. But, at times, she also encounters similar treatment from elderly Chinese people, who might walk up to her with a question. She wryly states that she is more forgiving of them since it is more likely that they have very little education and can hardly speak English.

Furthermore, Thanaletchmi sees her Hindu upbringing as a crucial part of her identity as an Indian. As her adoptive parents were devout Hindus, she slipped quite naturally into Hinduism. Growing up in a Hindu household meant that observing the Hindu festivals and practising day-to-day Hindu rituals were second nature to her. As a child, every year her adoptive father participated in the Thaipusam festival, commemorating Lord Murugan, the son of Shiva—one of the three most important gods in Hinduism. She not only accompanied him to this festival, but there were many years when she took a vow and joined the celebration herself by carrying the milk pot or the *paal kudam* and asked for forgiveness or offered thanks to Lord Murugan. Even after her adoptive father's passing, she continues to practise some Hindu rituals till this day. She always fasts before *Deepavali*—the festival of lights celebrated by Hindus to remember the spiritual victory of light over darkness.

The withering away of de facto child adoptions

Although the Adoption of Children Act 1939 that was already in effect might have led some to believe that formal adoptions became increasingly prevalent, especially in the 1960s with Singapore's independence and as the state gradually asserted more power in people's lives, but that was not the case. There were pockets of couples who still received transferred children into their lives although the numbers of these de facto 'adoptions' began to slowly decline. As in the past, however, during this time people used their own initiative or resources for tapping into family or personal networks—as it was in the case of Thanaletchmi's adoptive mother—to receive a transferred child. For couples like Thanaletchmi's adoptive parents, the opportunity of being presented a child through personal contacts would have been the only way to receive a child into their lives. Having a formal adoption would have been impossible, especially since they would not have had the resources to formally adopt a child. Nonetheless, as in all the other transferred or adopted children, Thanaletchmi's fate as a transferred child was to be a positive one. She led a happy and fulfilled life as she was very much loved and treasured by her adoptive parents.

Chapter 14

Treated the Same

Migration to Singapore

In the Malay community, child transfers occurred mostly amongst relatives. If a couple desiring a child could not acquire the child of a relative, there was the option of adopting a Chinese child. Many Malay families adopted Chinese girls. The Chinese had a built-in bias towards giving away their girl children while keeping their sons. However, the Malays did not have a preference for one sex over the other. Maah Mohamad Nadir was one such child. She was received into a Boyanese family as an infant. But many details about her adoption, as well as details about her own biological family, are unknown to her.

Her adoptive father had come to Singapore from Pulau Bawean, an island in East Java just north of Surabaya, in the late 1920s as a teenager in search of employment. Amongst the Boyanese, *merantau*, or the cultural tradition of men leaving their homes in search of money for the family, was practised. In fact, there was a growing number of Boyanese arriving in Singapore between 1901 and 1911, most likely because of a land tax imposed on them by the Dutch, which pushed many to leave for places like Singapore where jobs were in abundance.

Working as a driver was a typical occupation for many Boyanese men. Maah's adoptive father married her adoptive mother in the late 1920s. Unlike him, she came from a Boyanese family in Penang. For some years, however, they were childless. In her adulthood, Maah would learn from her adoptive mother that she had tried many times to conceive but failed as each pregnancy ended in a miscarriage. But as for why Maah was given away and how she had come to be adopted, those details of her life were never discussed. The only information she had was that she was born in 1934. She did not even know her birth date. All her legal documents, such as her identity card (IC), record her birthday as 1 January 1934 since her adoptive parents did not have the actual information regarding her birth and other details.

Discovering the truth about her adoption

Maah grew up as an only child for several years. When she was around seven to eight years old, while lying in bed one day, it was by accident that she overheard her adoptive parents talking to some guests in the living room of their home about her adoption. Little did her adoptive parents know that she had been eavesdropping on their conversation. They assumed she was fast asleep, taking her afternoon nap in the bedroom, as it was the case every day. But hearing about her adoption and learning that her adoptive parents were not her 'real' parents did not change how she saw her relationship with them. If anything, she felt an immense gratitude towards them for loving and caring for her.

Her realization about her adoption was sparked by another experience she had while growing up. She discovered that whenever she went shopping with her parents, the shopkeepers, as well as others around her, would frequently ask if she was adopted, since her skin colour was much lighter than that of her adoptive parents and she had slit eyes. In response, her adoptive parents would dismiss the comment and insist that Maah was their own child. Their response only delighted her as she found security in the fact that her adoptive parents saw her as their own.

As the years passed, not once did Maah inquire of her adoptive parents about her biological parents. She did not desire to go in search of her biological parents nor was she interested in knowing how she came to be given away by them. For her, the fact of her adoption was a non-issue. This was the case with many child transfers involving Chinese infants adopted into Malay families. Very seldom did the biological and adoptive families keep in touch, especially when the adoptive child was a non-Malay. If they did, the Malay parent would take the child to the biological family's home during Chinese New Year. It was common for the child to be given an *angpow*, a gift of money in a red packet. In turn, on Hari Raya, the biological parents would visit the home of the couple adopting their daughter. But in most instances, ties were cut off early in the child's life. This was so that the child would not be encouraged to seek her biological relatives since by then warm attachments would have already developed between the adopted child and her adoptive parents. Thus, an adoptive parent would prefer a complete severance of ties between the child and the birth parents. This would also give the adoptive parents full, independent parental control over the transferred child.

Second World War

Then came the Japanese occupation which caused an upheaval in the family. While many Boyanese had left Bawean Island rather than starve there, Maah recalls that her adoptive parents decided to return to the island to be with family as soon as the War started, just before the sailing ships ceased to operate. Having to leave Singapore meant that Maah had to stop her schooling at the *madrasah*—religious school—where she studied Arabic for a year. It was not known if they had decided to return thinking that Bawean Island was a much safer place to be at during the Second World War. Maah's adoptive father had relatives residing there. Or it might be that they felt safer fleeing Singapore since the

Japanese were targeting the Chinese, including Chinese children. Back on Bawean Island, as a little girl, Maah remembers her adoptive parents living off the family farm when they returned to live with their relatives—they, together with their relatives, would work in their gardens, planting vegetables and other food crops to survive. When the Japanese occupation ended in 1945, she and her adoptive parents returned to Singapore since it was in Singapore that her father could find waged work.

Living in a pondok

On arriving in Singapore, the family took up residence in a *pondok* or lodging house, called Pondok Tachgan, near Clemenceau Avenue. It was one of several *pondoks*, the largest of which was at Kampong Kapor, known to the Malays as Kampong Boyan. Although she was young, she remembers very clearly that around fourteen or fifteen families resided in each *pondok*, with each family having their own sleeping area separated by curtains. There was a shared kitchen and shared toilet for everyone to utilize. For the Boyanese, the *pondok* was more than a residential feature; it was a social institution, since communal living was meant to help the newly arrived migrants in the Boyanese community to settle down in a foreign land. But more importantly, a *pondok* was organized along the *desa* or village in Bawean Island so that the newly arrived migrants would be able to quickly settle in. By the 1950s, there were over a hundred of these lodging houses throughout Singapore. These dwellings were differentiated from a *kampong* since the houses in a *kampong* were constructed out of *atap* roofs and wood. But a *pondok* was always made of brick and cement. Pondok Gelam at Club Street was the last *pondok* in Singapore. Cleared in 2000, it was later designated as a historic site.

All the families residing in the *pondok* where Maah and her adoptive parents stayed were of Boyanese descent. Maah stood out since she was of Chinese descent. There was one woman

who called her out one day for her being Chinese. The fact
of her Chinese origin could not be erased because of her light
skin tone, which was viewed favourably amongst many Asians,
including Indonesians and Malays, who tended to have a darker
skin tone. A light skin tone, however, counted as an advantage
in child transfers since a fair-skin tone was considered beautiful.
Although Maah brushed off that incident, it was obvious that
people around her knew implicitly that she was not of Boyanese
descent. But no one in the *pondok* or the surrounding *pondoks*
whom her parents had gotten to know over the years would
inquire about Maah's background. Were they trying to be polite?
Or was it a case of their knowing that she was adopted but
treating her as they would treat any Boyanese person? This could
have stemmed from the idea, prevalent amongst them, as well as
the Malays, that a non-Boyanese or non-Malay could assimilate
into the community as long as they spoke the Boyanese language
and was Muslim.

The arrival of a 'sibling'

It was around this time that Maah's adoptive mother had a son.
In 1945, Masrohen arrived. Being the only child of her adoptive
parents, they loved him dearly. For Maah's adoptive parents, the
family structure was now complete—it was perfect since they had
a boy and a girl, exemplifying a complementary gender balance.
It was not that they were reluctant to receive girls. Girls were
welcomed, especially since the Malays—and elderly Malay couples
more so—knew that girls would stay around and would be useful
to an ageing couple. They could cook, wash clothes, and do other
household chores. More than that, girls were good companions
and would never desert their parents unlike boys. After getting
married, sons were more likely to be concerned with the affairs of
their own families, including providing for them.

In spite of the joy Masrohen had brought to the couple, there was never even one instance in which they gave him more attention than they gave Maah. In fact, Maah would continue to be showered with love and affection, as if she was the only child. Her adoptive parents were even more protective of her because she was a girl. She does not remember leaving the house unaccompanied even once. Unlike other young girls who had friends from school, to Maah, her entire world would only comprise her adoptive parents and her adoptive brother.

Growing up, the bond they all shared was very close as they were a close-knit family. Maah remembers getting along well with everyone in the family and there was no sibling rivalry between Maah and her adoptive brother. However, as a young boy, Masrohen was playful and enjoyed teasing Maah whenever he could, even to the extent that some of the comments hurled at her were caustic. He was the 'type' who hardly minced his words. There was one painful incident, however, which Maah would never forget. Realizing that Maah was not his 'real' sister, even though he had been told by his parents that she was his 'sister', one day he blurted out the 'fact' of her adoption, only to receive the disapproval of his own parents. While not knowing what triggered his response, Maah did not think much of the incident after it occurred because she had an implicit understanding that her adoptive parents never saw her as an 'outsider' to the family. In fact, the only thing she recalls was how her adoptive mother chided him for his actions and reminded him never ever to bring up the matter again. To this day, she feels 'fortunate' that her adoptive parents have always 'been on her side' even though she was not their biological child.

Maah was around twelve years old by then. Because she had to get her identity card (IC) done, she recalls accompanying her father to an office not far from Killiney Road where they lived. In her memory, her father did not have to present any legal documentation related to her adoption. As soon as they sat down, the enumerator quickly recorded her details: her full name and place of birth in accordance with the information presented to him by her adoptive father. As for her race, the enumerator wrote down 'Malay'. This was not an error, especially since many of Boyanese extraction intermarried and assimilated into the Malay community on settling down in Singapore.

Her marriage

For Maah, the return to Singapore ushered in a significant rite of passage for her. On turning fifteen, she had several suitors, but there was one Ibrahim Haji Idrus who took a fancy to her, although there was a twenty-year gap between them. Typically, it was not uncommon for girls to marry while in their teens, especially if they were not educated enough or if they were not working. Introduced by her father's relative, Ibrahim came from Java to Singapore, also in search of employment. In their forty-four-year marriage, Maah and her husband had ten children altogether—the eldest when she was nineteen and the youngest when she was forty-one years of age. Soon, there were twenty grandchildren and twenty-one great grandchildren added to the extended family. For all her married life, Maah was a homemaker while her husband was a taxi driver, driving the black and yellow cabs typical of Singapore from the 1950s to the 1980s.

In her marriage to Ibrahim, there was never an instance in which the fact of her adoption or her being 'Chinese' came up. They entered into the Malay community in every respect and produced children of their own, sometimes having noticeably lighter skin and prominent Chinese features. As in most *anak angkat* (Malay, literally meaning 'raised child'), Maah was implicitly a Malay woman in every way—she dressed in a *sarong kebaya,* spoke Malay, and cooked Malay fare. And more importantly for Maah's husband, she was a Muslim.

But what seemed to attract others' attention in her marriage to Ibrahim was not the fact that she was of a different 'race' but the fact that she was 'very young'—an obvious fact given the differences in their appearance. In those days, child brides were not uncommon in the Malay community. As soon as a girl came of age, she was quickly married off with the expectation that she would look after the house and raise a brood of children. It was also commonplace for some poor families to 'sell' daughters, if they could not feed them, although this did not occur amongst the Malays as much as it did amongst the Chinese. While the twenty-year gap between Maah and her husband seemed to turn heads, it must be highlighted that young teenage girls were sometimes married off to men who could be the ages of their fathers or even grandfathers, being thirty or forty years older than them. Frequently, these marriages had disastrous consequences for these girls who would choose to run away from their husbands. But Maah's marriage was a happy one, in spite of the considerable age difference. Her husband was a simple man who did not make unreasonable demands of her. She also recalls being treated with great respect, and her husband was appreciative of whatever she did for the family.

Her adoptive family

Soon after her marriage, her adoptive parents passed on. First, it was her adoptive mother in 1962, followed by her adoptive father in 1977. Although these were very sad times in her life, she discovered another dimension of their love for her—that they would always treat her no differently from their one and only biological son. On her adoptive mother's death, Maah received a large piece of gold jewellery from her which she treasures till today. Masrohen, too, would go on to receive a small inheritance—a gift of money left behind by her adoptive father. It was not a large sum, given her adoptive father was not a wealthy man.

In spite of being adopted, she would never be seen as an outsider by her only adoptive brother. Until he passed on in 2012, they would visit each other regularly. Even their children have developed a deep mutual bond. For Maah, the beauty of her adoption lay in the fact that her adoptive parents never treated her differently from their only son. It was not important that she does not know who her biological relatives were. It was also not important that the fact of her adoption was kept hidden from her. For her, the only thing that really mattered was that she was nurtured and guarded by a couple who loved her deeply.

A studio photo taken in 1956 with Maah, her adoptive parents, her adoptive brother, Masrohen, her husband, Ibrahim, and her two oldest children.

Chapter 15

An Exception to the Rule

Growing up a Malay boy

Splashed across the front page of *The New Paper*, a local Singapore newspaper, in November 2015 was an article featuring an adoptee. It was an account of a grassroots community activist and leader and his search for his roots. Raised in a Malay family, Fahmi Rais was quite old when he discovered that he was adopted. To be exact, he was in his mid-forties. What is distinct about his story is that he represents an outlier. In the past, girls formed the majority of children who were given away. It was a rarity for boys to be given up through adoption.

Born in 1967 and raised since infancy in a middle-class Malay home, Fahmi was the adopted son of Ahmad Mohamad Rais, a religious teacher or *ustad* at the mosque situated in the old Indonesian Embassy, once standing along Orchard Road, in addition to working in the finance department of the embassy. His active participation in community life included his role as the principal of the Muslim boy's orphanage along Mattar Road at one time. Coming from a prominent family of *ustads*, Fahmi's adoptive father's own father was the *imam*—the person who leads prayers—of the Sultan Mosque located in historic Kampong Glam, where the Muslim community in Singapore would congregate. His siblings were all religious teachers as well. Unlike his adoptive father, his adoptive mother led a more homebound life as she was mainly a homemaker.

Like other adopted children, Fahmi became gradually integrated into the Malay community since childhood. His parents being steeped in Islam meant that Fahmi was raised observing the pillars and tenets of Islam. Growing up, Fahmi learned to fast, recognizing it as an important part of his being a Muslim. At the age of five, he started off by fasting for a quarter of a day. Then it was half a day when he was six years old. He proudly declares having achieved 'a full one day fast' when he was seven years of age. At the age of eight, he accompanied his parents to Mecca for the holy pilgrimage. Although he learned very little Arabic himself, finding it a very difficult language to master, he learned the discipline of praying five times a day, remembering all the important prayers and their meanings.

Being the only child in the family, his parents loved him dearly. He had a happy childhood and enjoyed school, first attending Mattar East Primary School, followed by Woodsville Primary School and then Woodsville Secondary School. As a little boy in Primary One, Fahmi had vivid memories of how his mother walked him to school every day. Each day she would wait at the gate religiously until she heard the first recess bell. Only then would she start walking home, which was unlike what most other mothers did, he observed. She would faithfully pack him his food every day. She did this fearing that he might not have anything to eat during recess time should the queues be too long. Fahmi has good memories of his school days, although he was teased for looking like a Chinese by his classmates who would call him 'Ah Chong' in jest. He also read Chinese as a second language since his mother had the foresight to recognize that he would be better off studying an additional language, given that he was already fluent in Malay. Fahmi took Malay as a second language only when he entered Woodsville Primary School.

The change in school was brought about when the family moved from Mattar Road to Sims Drive.

He then went on to pursue degrees in law and mass communications, was appointed to senior positions in multinational corporations, before taking the plunge and starting up two advertising, marketing, and public relations agencies. His career in communications led him to launch two Malay channels—Prime 12, which was a free-to-air channel where he also supervised the Indian programming, in 1995, followed by Sensasi, a cable channel, in 2007. Fahmi's highest appointment in MediaCorp was as Vice President of Suria Programming and Promotions Network. There, he initiated several new milestones for the channel, including the start of the Malay Artistes Management Unit. As his passion for communications evolved, he chose to manage his own entertainment productions business under the Raistar brand.

Following in the footsteps of his father, Fahmi later became active in the community life of Singapore from 1991 to 2011. He started off by being the student councillor with the Institute of Education before becoming the chairman of the Islamic Fellowship Youth Wing. He then held the position of vice president of the Central Council of Malay Cultural Organisations Singapore (*Majlis Pusat*). After this, he was board member of Mendaki and National Youth Council. He then became the Secretary-General of the Southeast Asia Muslim Youth Organisation (SAMYO), an organization comprising more than three million members. His experience in community work enabled him to start several other NGOs, including the Johor-Singapore Community Care Association, Puan Noor Aishah Intercultural Institute, and the Association for Trainers, Educators and Mentors (A. TEAM).

Earlier on in his career, he also lectured at a tuition centre. It was there that he met his future wife Sulaimah Bte Abdul Kadir, whom he married in 1995. They have four wonderful children, one of whom is a girl, whom they have adopted.

Realization about his adoption

In his childhood, there was never a time when he thought he was adopted. Although not at all resembling his parents, who had a much darker skin tone, he always thought he was a part of the family and his fairer skin colouring was more like his cousins. To his knowledge, he was aware that they had been adopted and were possibly Chinese. But he did not connect that idea to himself or suspect that he might also be adopted. There was nothing to push him in that direction until he was well into his adulthood.

From time to time, he received some vague comments from some distant relatives who made no secret of 'his adoption'. It left him puzzled, especially since his parents did not breathe a word to him about the matter, even taking 'the truth' with them on their passing. One day, he decided to ask his adoptive mother about it, but her only remark was, 'Don't believe everything you hear . . . and what these people are saying . . . you see, look at your birth certificate . . . doesn't it show that we are your parents?' Because his adoptive mother could be described as 'a lioness and was very fierce and that no one dared question her', he decided to erase the matter from his mind. Although his attention turned to other things, it only lasted for a very short while. Before long, he was troubled again by his longing to know about his roots. The idea that he might possibly be adopted had already been planted in his mind.

In fact, there were several incidents which led him to believe that he might not be the 'real' child of his adoptive parents. Fahmi's adoptive father was an avid photographer. But in all the photographs he had seen, which his adoptive father safely kept away for many years, nowhere could he find his mother pregnant with him. He recalls that all of them showed his adoptive mother in her younger days without a child, or Fahmi as a very young toddler or as a teenage boy holding his adoptive mother's hand. He was also curious as to why his uncles and aunts were so keen on getting him married to an adoptive cousin of his after the demise of his parents. For him, it seemed extremely odd, especially since they grew up together. In hindsight, having him married to one of his 'adoptive relatives' could have been a way his adoptive close relatives were trying to 'turn him into a family member' by having him transformed into an affinal relative, at the least. Then, there was the touchy incident of the sale of his adoptive parent's HDB (government-subsidized) flat. Not aware that he was adopted, he went ahead to sell the flat and kept the proceeds, which irked one of his adoptive uncles, since the Islamic inheritance laws did not permit an adopted child to automatically receive a legacy. Because that adoptive uncle could not lay claim to the flat, which was left in Fahmi's name, it was not surprising that he appeared at the flat, unbeknownst to him, during his mother's funeral and took away much of his mother's jewellery. This too would go on to ferment Fahmi's doubting mind.

It was business as usual after those incidents until life took a turn one fateful day—his adoptive grandmother on his adoptive mother's side told him the startling truth. Fahmi was forty-five years of age at that time. Before her death, he plucked up the courage and asked her the question that had been troubling him for some time. 'I hear people who claim that I'm adopted . . . That's not true, right, grandma?' When there was a long pause, and she failed to reply, he knew instantly what that silence meant. It confirmed every fear and suspicion that he had harboured about his parentage, triggering a cascade of emotions. In that same incident, he was to find out that his Chinese mother was from Segamat in the Johor state of peninsular Malaysia. This could very well have been true since travel between Singapore and Malaysia was not restricted after 1965, in spite of Singapore having been separated from Malaysia at that time. There was no need for a passport, and there were no check points until July 1967, when blue passports were issued to cross into Malaysia or vice versa. Thus, adopting a child in Malaysia and bringing him or her back into Singapore would not have been too difficult. But there was another piece of information that troubled him even more—discovering that his biological parents were so poor that they had requested some money in exchange for him. To him, that was as good as being 'sold', not even given away, and he was extremely scarred by that discovery.

Hurt, feeling betrayed, and alienated

A few more years would pass after the truth about his adoption had been unearthed. Far from feeling settled having learned the truth from his adoptive grandmother, in the immediate months, Fahmi was pushed to the brink of crisis, and his life was thrown into disarray. He was hurt from knowing that he was 'not the product of his parent's love'. His longing to be their one and only child, since they were childless for ten years before Fahmi came along, ran very deep. This was coupled with the fact of having been raised by them for forty-five years. His sense of alienation was amplified by the fact that people whom he had thought were 'family' all these decades were, in actuality, not his kin. Moreover, another shock was that all of his relatives, cousins included, knew that he had been adopted but chose to keep the matter quiet. For him, trying to reconcile with the thought of being an 'outsider' to his adoptive family and not their 'real child' was too painful to bear.

The whole incident hit Fahmi so badly that he was forced into questioning his very identity. Up to that point, his entire identity had been based on believing that the family he had grown up in was his own. That idea, however, was completely shattered. He began to question everything. Overcome with a sense of betrayal, he felt strongly that his adoptive parents should not have kept such an important detail of his life away from him. The night when the truth was made known to him, Fahmi cried in the arms of his wife and children. He just could not reconcile his present and his past.

In the immediate months to come, Fahmi battled depression. Although friends advised him 'to snap out' of the situation he was in, he found it difficult to do so. Instead, he thought if he could create a new identity for himself, that might help him cope with the pain. So, for a good five years or so, Fahmi decided to take on the name of Rayan Daniyal, legally changing his birth name. The name he adopted was non-Malay for a reason. It was a conscious effort on his part to help him detach himself from his adoptive Malay roots. After all, he had discovered that he was not Malay. Although knowing that he was Chinese by birth, he decided against a Chinese name since he did not know if he was a 'Tan, Lee, or Lim.' But neither did he choose a Christian name. Instead, a name cloaked in ambivalence was the most logical to him, since he was Chinese, while growing up as a Malay, and simultaneously being a Muslim. Surprisingly, that name change would help him immensely to cope with the emotional trauma that he was going through, but only for a brief period.

To satisfy his yearning to know the truth, Fahmi ended up in the Family Court, going through adoption documents, blueprints, and everything else he could get his hands on, to get to the 'bottom of his adoption'. At about the same time, he approached the Immigration and Checkpoints Authority (ICA) of Singapore to try to change his racial status on his identity card. He was intent on changing his race from Malay to Chinese. However, he was thwarted by the fact that the immigration officer told him that attempts to change race required parental consent, which was impossible for Fahmi, since his adoptive parents had already passed on.

Watching him from afar all this while were his adoptive cousins. Seeing his frustration and learning about his struggles with his identity, they were quick to respond. They insisted that he should accept his journey in life and recognize what his adoptive parents did for him. He was reminded of the love they had for him. Although he accepted their advice to move on and not make a fuss about his adoption, their relationship was never as warm and cordial as before. Over the years, Fahmi did not communicate with them as frequently as before, and the relationship he had with them began to weaken gradually, as if experiencing a slow death.

His birth certificate

Why it had taken so long for him to discover the truth about his adoption was something Fahmi himself pondered over. He had never suspected he was adopted since his adoptive parents' names appeared on his birth certificate, leading him to believe that they were his birth parents. Furthermore, he resembled his cousins, who presumably were adopted, and thus there was no reason for him to believe otherwise in terms of his parentage. The difference, however, was that he was never told he was adopted while they were told that they were. Fahmi surmised that the reason for their knowing that they were adopted could have been that they had 'adoptive siblings'. Telling a child that he or she was adopted was important because of Islamic rules surrounding inheritance—an adoptive child is not entitled to any inheritance that any biological child could receive. In Fahmi's case, he was the only child, and thus there was no necessity for his adoptive parents to reveal the truth about his adoption.

Today with a sober face, Fahmi suspects that his birth certificate might have even been 'doctored', especially since it documents his place of birth as Kandang Kerbau Hospital, assuming that his adoptive grandmother was telling him the truth that he was born in Segamat. He would later find out that the written statement of his birth was processed in the early 1970s, although he had been born in 1967, further throwing suspicion on the details reflected in his birth certificate. At the same time, he would learn that his adoptive parents sought a lawyer to process the adoption— another fact he discovered much later in his life. Rather than being a transferred child, there is the possibility that Fahmi was an adopted child since his parents went through the legal process of having him adopted by them. But because the 'facts' on his birth certificate might not have been true, that too posed a hurdle since it has made it harder for him to trace his roots.

Preference for a son

There is one distinct fact that sets Fahmi's adoption apart from the bulk of the child adoptions that took place from the late 1920s to the 1970s in Singapore. In Singapore's past, girls formed the majority of the children who were given up for adoption. Far fewer boys were transferred, and thus adopted, compared with girls. If boys were transferred, it was usually because a member of the family had taken ill, or the child was ill himself. So, it was thought that the boy child brought on bad luck and had to be immediately transferred out of the birth family. But, in reality, male infants were seldom transferred as sons were treasured. This whole idea of boys being precious had a great influence on decisions made around whether a child should be given up for adoption.

There are several Asian cultures which are known to be notoriously patriarchal, characterized by men being in a privileged position compared to women. Male dominance is expressed in different ways. Chinese culture holds fast to the idea of preferring a son, as does Indian culture. For the Chinese, a man's family takes precedence over the woman's. So, a woman always marries into her husband's family—she takes on her husband's name on marriage and looks after the ancestral tablet of her husband's family. In Indian culture, a similar preference for boys is held.

Sons are favoured since, in the Hindu death rituals, a son is needed to conduct the last rites of the deceased. However, the Chinese and the Indians differ in one respect when it comes to adoption. Giving up of children occur much less amongst the Indians than it does amongst the Chinese.

In Asia, the practice of preferring a son goes back many centuries. The phrase 'boys are precious, girls are a burden' describes Chinese and Indian cultures all too well. It is deeply entrenched in the psyche of the people of these cultures and ideas related to preferring a son were brought with them as they migrated to Southeast Asia. While being held strongly amongst the older generations in Singapore, the idea is virtually non-existent amongst those who are younger.

The mystery of his adoption

But if sons were precious to the Chinese, why was Fahmi given away? A lead came from amongst his adoptive relatives on his adoptive father's side. He mentioned in passing that Fahmi's biological mother died in childbirth, and he had to be given away. But Fahmi was hesitant to accept this response. It seemed like a way of forcing him to accept the fact of his adoption, find closure, and not attempt to find his biological relatives. And because that information could not be verified, he was forced to let it go eventually.

That question, however, troubled him for many years to come. And it remains a question to which he may never find an answer to this day. It appears that only his adoptive parents knew his biological parents. But all those years, they suppressed the details of Fahmi's adoption, not sharing any information with anyone else except perhaps with his adoptive maternal grandmother. Unfortunately, even that little information he uncovered could not be verified.

Like some adoptive children, he underwent an intense period of wanting to seek out his biological relatives. This occurred a few years after the revelation of his adoption. There were two [several] distinct attempts: first in Malaysia and then in Singapore. Thinking that he could find his relatives in Johor, Fahmi granted press interviews and his story was covered by Chinese newspapers in both Singapore and Malaysia. But the outcome was disappointing—no one came forward. Then there was *The New Paper*, a Singapore-based newspaper in tabloid form, that featured a piece on him. Standing as a Malay candidate for an opposition party in the general elections of 2015, Fahmi felt that they had exploited the situation by reporting that the 'Malay candidate (that is, Fahmi) was actually Chinese'. This discredited him and placed him in a precarious position as he had contested in the General Election of 2015 in the Tanjong Pagar GRC (group representation constituency) under the banner of the Singaporeans First party. That too did not lead to anything concrete. Another opportunity emerged when he went on air on *Channel News Asia* radio. Soon after the programme, his heart skipped a beat when the station received a call that someone had responded to his story. But unfortunately, the person calling in was born in 1966 and not 1967! Once again, he encountered a dead end.

Accepting the truth about his adoption

With the passage of time, Fahmi decided to revert to using his original name, given to him by his adoptive parents. He has come to respect his adoptive parents, realizing that although it was painful to learn that they had kept the truth from him, they must have had his best interests at heart. Since he was a prominent figure within the Malay community, it helped immensely that many of his friends affirmed his Malay identity and never once questioned it.

He was consoled by many of his peers that since he had lived his life thus far as a Malay by speaking the Malay language, adopting the Malay culture, and embracing Islam as his religion, he is, in every sense, a Malay. Many echoed the same message—'Fahmi, not to worry. As far as I am concerned, you are 100 per cent Malay.' This message was amplified again and again, and, interestingly, not one person in the community uttered the words 'Good thing you know your roots now.' While the Malay community embraced him 'as one of them', he did not think he would receive the same, cordial, inclusive reception from the Chinese community.

Today, Fahmi is more settled in his emotions about his adoption. Being more mature and letting time do its part in healing the hurt had a big part to play in his accepting his adoption. In the spirit of helping others in the community, who may be in the same situation that he had found himself in, he started a support group for adopted children seeking answers about their adoption. Setting up a Facebook page, he hoped to meet others in his situation, with the express purpose of drawing strength from each other. Unfortunately, his plan of bringing others from a similar background and experience together failed as the Facebook page did not draw any response. The idea was dropped as a result.

Coming to terms with his own adoption, he has made it a point to be open with his adopted daughter about her roots. As he was hurt from learning that he was an adopted child at a much older age, he concludes, 'It is always important to tell the truth . . . adopted children deserve to know the truth . . . holding to the principle that you always have to come out clean.'

Leaving behind the traumatic period he went through when he battled with his emotions regarding his adoption, Fahmi now jokes about his background. He says that he is the most 'politically correct Singaporean'—Chinese by birth, Malay by upbringing, and has an Indian wife, having had the 'lived experience' of all the three major ethnic groups. His positive outlook is expressed in yet another way. He has managed to overcome the tensions arising from his inability to locate his biological family and discovering that his adoptive parents had concealed the truth of his adoption from him for a good many years. Instead, now he openly acknowledges the 'good life' his adoptive parents had given him and that he might not have been the person he is today without having been given away. In other words, he accepts his adoption as being God's design for his life and believes that it was meant to be.

Fahmi and his adoptive parents. This is a studio photo taken on his first birthday, 23 December 1968.

Photo taken with Fahmi's adoptive parents in Mecca in 1975. This was Fahmi's first overseas trip and their first pilgrimage together as a family.

Epilogue

The 1960s saw a gradual rise in formal adoptions. During this time, children were received into their adoptive families through legal arrangements. In other words, the transfer of a child entailed the intervention of the state and the laws of the country. If formal transfers of children did occur prior to this period, more often than not, the adoption fees were shouldered by the wealthier families. Details of such cases are few and far between. Formally adopting a child ensures that the child could be protected so that he or she might not be 'adopted' for other purposes. An example would be when the child was adopted to become the bride of one of the sons in the family. Another instance would be a family adopting a child only to have her provide domestic labour in the family. This was especially so right up to the late 1960s. Up until that time, children could be adopted for any number of reasons and not just for the sole purpose of having the child become a part of the family. And so, at that time, relatively few adoptions strictly followed the arrangements specified under law.

But the late 1960s onwards proved to be an interesting time for couples wishing to adopt. In essence, there was an explosion of formal adoptions while de facto adoptions became a thing of the past. Essentially, this meant that the state had a greater say in children being transferred from one family to another. Paradoxically, by that time, the number of children available for adoption plunged as births started to decline. Generally, the decades ahead were marked by long queues of childless couples waiting anxiously to adopt a child. Also, at this time, it was no longer poverty or cultural beliefs that pushed people to give up their children. If there were couples or individuals intending to give the child away, the mothers usually had them out of wedlock. This was before contraception and abortion became available. And so, women had to surrender their children for adoption.

The more salient feature of this period was that cross-cultural adoptions came to a halt. The hand of the state was involved in this decision, leading to a turn of events. A small committee was formed in 1972, and everyone in it, becoming the architect of change, agreed that prospective adoptive parents could not adopt children from outside their own ethnic group. Hence, Indian couples could only adopt Indian children. The same applied to the Malays and the Chinese.

The reason for this change in the adoption law was hotly debated by officers working in government. In spite of the joys of adopting a child, adoptions can prove to be challenging and complex. Members of the committee felt that the experience of being adopted is already traumatic for the children. To add another layer of complication—of being adopted outside one's ethnic group—would be doubly traumatizing for the child on discovering that their parents, whom they grew up thinking were theirs, were, in reality, not related to them. This would be especially painful for children to handle if they were in their teenage years—a time in a child's life which is often fairly unsettling. And if the child is upset at his or her adoptive parents, the child might not come to respect them.

In an Asian setting like Singapore, things can get more complicated, especially when parents do not want to reveal the fact about the adoption to the child. Although being loving and caring towards the child, it is wishful thinking to expect adoptive parents of the past to tell the child the truth. Many were probably fearful as to how the child would receive the truth, assuming that it might hurt the child's feelings, since it can be a deeply unsettling episode in his or her life. Others could have decided to 'keep mum' about the adoption, seeing it as potentially disruptive to the relationship they might have established with the child. Fearing that the child may go in search of his or her birth parents and abandon his or her adoptive parents was a constant existential threat to many adoptive parents. It is not surprising then that adoptive parents have been found to use a menu of tricks to conceal the real identity of the child, some far-fetched and incomprehensible, others demonstrably false. It is only in rare cases that the truth comes to light and adoptive parents openly inform the child about his or her adoption.

The final decision to let the child know that he or she is adopted lies with the adoptive parents. They have to weigh the pros and cons of revealing the information to the child. If the parents do want to tell the child that he or she is adopted, it is ideal to do so when the child is young as it would give the child enough time to process his or her emotions as the child gains self-awareness during his or her formative years. And by extension, the child is less likely to get upset since they know they are loved—an experience validated in real time. In fact, if the child finds out the truth from someone other than his or her parents, they can at best regard this as egregious behaviour on the part their parents, and at worst find it emotionally damaging.

Looking back at Singapore's past, it cannot be argued that adoption has always provided a 'forever family' and permanent home for many children, from the late 1920s right up to the 1960s. As the idea of adopting a child outside of one's ethnic community began to die out, adoptions within the ethnic community became the norm in the early 1970s. However, to have the court make the adoption legal was costly. And so, what dictated adoptions was the financial capability of the couple desiring a child. As more people began to accumulate wealth, adoptions became increasingly possible. Since couples wanting to receive a child did so through adoptions rather than transfers, the idea of a transferred child began to fade from the collective memory of Singaporeans. The idea of a transferred child became a phenomenon of the past, etched in the collective memory of the older generation, never to repeat itself.

Acknowledgements

I have had a twenty-year adventure of studying the forces of history, culture, ethnicity, and religion and their profound influence on child adoption and transfers in Singapore. Many people have contributed to the rich knowledge I have acquired over the years.

In this collection of biographies, I have tried to serve as the voice for a handful of adoptees who have been willing to share their stories of adoption with me so generously. In particular, I wish to thank all the adoptees whose personal stories have been featured in this book and the hours they spent with me relating the details of their lives as adopted children. They have been so kind, so patient, so wise, and, most of all, so forthcoming about their lives—sharing with me, a total stranger, the joys and struggles they have gone through as adopted children. They have even carefully rechecked their stories after they had been written. I can't thank each one of them enough.

While researching for this book, I have had the unique opportunity of speaking to some people whose knowledge of the topic of child adoption and child transfers was especially illuminating. Two individuals I wish to acknowledge are Laurence Wee and M. Subramaniam, both of whom worked as welfare officers in the Singapore government from the 1960s and early 1970s onwards respectively.

The experience of writing this book was a formidable one, especially since I had not written a book of a similar nature before. For supporting me and so painstakingly combing the manuscript and commenting on it, I would like to acknowledge Kana Gopal. She has massively contributed to some of the ideas presented in the stories. Aside from her role in shaping this book, I would also like to thank her for our wonderful friendship.

I would also like to acknowledge the support of family and friends, including my brother, John Wilson Devasahayam, who fact- and spell-checked the biographies included in this book. Also to be thanked is Umaira Farouk, whose contributions towards the archival research for this book were immensely valuable, and I deeply appreciate her efforts. Thanks also go to Elizabeth Wright for proofreading the manuscript. Any errors arising in this book are only mine.

I am also indebted to Eva Wong Nava for leading me to Penguin Random House and to Tim Yap Fuan who enabled me to conduct archival research at the National University of Singapore Library.

Also, I am grateful to my friend Thavamani Ratnasamy, whose intense encouragement pushed me to embark on the writing in spite of all the odds stacked against me in the initial stages. I wish to thank Low Chiou Yeong and Sunita Singh for the same reason.

And finally, voluminous thanks to Nora Nazerene Abu Bakar for her perseverance in chasing me for the manuscript after reading the proposal I had sent her months before starting on the book and her design and editorial team at Penguin Random House responsible for the cover design and for bringing this book to its final form.

Theresa W. Devasahayam
15 October 2023

References

'A Century of Cinemas, Movies and Blockbusters'. *Remember Singapore*. 2 August 2012. https://remembersingapore. org/2012/08/02/singapore-cinemas-history/.

'Adelphi Hotel at Coleman Street'. National Heritage Board. 4 April 2023. https://www.roots.gov.sg/Collection-Landing/ listing/1137840.

Cornelius, Vernon. 'High Street'. *Singapore Infopedia*. 2018. https://eresources.nlb.gov.sg/infopedia/articles/SIP_497_ 2004-12-15.html.

Crinis, Vicki D. 'Sex Trafficking to the Federated Malay States 1920–1940: From Migration for Prostitution to Victim or Criminal?' *The Journal of Imperial and Commonwealth History*, 2019, 48(2): 296–318.

Devasahayam, Theresa W. 'Abandoned Daughters: Child Adoption by Indian Families in Pre-Independence Malaya and Singapore'. *Journal of the Malaysian Branch of the Royal Asiatic Society (JMBRAS)*, 2020 93(319): 137–52.

Jaschok, Maria. *Concubines and Bondservants: The Social History of a Chinese Custom*. Zed Books, 1988.

'Labouring to Deliver: A History of Kandang Kerbau Hospital'. *BiblioAsia*. April–June, 2022. https://biblioasia.nlb.gov.sg/ vol-18/issue-1/apr-to-jun-2022/history-kandang-kerbau-hospital/.

Leow, Annabeth. 'From Treating Sex Workers to Maternity Hospital: History of KKH'. *The Straits Times*, 17 October 2016. https://www.straitstimes.com/singapore/health/from-treating-sex-workers-to-maternity-hospital-history-of-kkh.

Leow, Rachel. '"Do You Own Non-Chinese Mui Tsai?" Re-examining Race and Female Servitude in Malaya and Hong Kong, 1919–1939'. *Modern Asian Studies*, 2012, 46(6): 1736–63.

Liu, Gretchen. 'Raffles Hotel & the Romance of Travel'. *BiblioAsia*. 1 October 2014. https://biblioasia.nlb.gov.sg/vol-10/issue-3/oct-dec-2014/raffles-hotel-singapore-history/.

'Most babies born in a Maternity Hospital—World Record'. Singapore Book of Records. https://singaporerecords.com/most-babies-born-in-a-maternity-hospital/#:~:text=KKH%20won%20a%20place%20in,100%20babies%20were%20delivered%20daily.

Ng, Kee Chong, Ho, Lai Yun, Quak, Seng Hock, Tan, Keng Wee, Ho, Nai Kiong, and Phua Kong Boo. 'From the 20th to the 21st century: The First 100 Years of Paediatrics in Singapore'. *Singapore Medical Journal*, 62 (1 Suppl): S2–S12, 2021, doi: 10.11622/smedj.2021068.

Ngoh, Heng Hong. 'The Adopted Child with Particular Reference to the Child Adopted into a Family of a Different Race', Research Paper, 2020, Department of Social Studies, University of Malaya.

Peterson, Jane A. 'Penang's Pearl: The Eastern & Oriental Hotel.' *Forbes Asia*, 3 October 2018. https://www.forbes.com/sites/forbesasia/2018/10/03/penangs-pearl-the-eastern-oriental-hotel/?sh=64f989b41653.

Tan, K. and S. Chern. 'Progress in Obstetrics from 19th to 21st Centuries: Perspectives from KK Hospital, Singapore—the Former World's Largest Maternity Hospital'. *The Internet Journal of Gynecology and Obstetrics*. 2002, 2(2): 1–15.

'U.S. Electronics Company Opens $6 million Singapore Subsidiary'. *Straits Times*. 4 July 1969, p.14.

Wee, Ann. *A Tiger Remembers: The Way We Were in Singapore*. Singapore: NUS Press.

Yee, Janet Keng Luan. National Archives Interview. 19 November 2007. Social Sector, Accession Number 003251, Reel/Disc 3, 00:58:40.